ASYLUM BOOKS

Soul Survivor

A journey of love, a journey of travel, a journey of suffering, a journey of knowledge a journey of joy, a journey of hope. Mary was a nun for seven years. On leaving the convent in 1972, within two years she had met and married her husband Jim. Within a further two years, she found herself in Sarsfield Court Psychiatric Hospital, two days after the birth of her daughter. Heavily medicated and subjected to many sessions of electro-convulsive therapy, it was the beginning of a nightmare that saw her admitted to a further three psychiatric hospitals - the GF wing of Cork University Hospital, St. Anne's in Cork and St. Patrick's in Dublin.

Blindly putting his trust in the 'experts', Jim acquiesced in all the treatment and he and Mary bought into what is now referred to as 'The Medical Model'. They were told that Mary had 'a chemical imbalance' in her brain that gave her a 'bi-polar mood disorder'. She was given the stigmatising label of 'manic-depressive'. In 1983, along with other medication she was already taking, she was put on lithium and told she would have to take it for the rest of her life, just as a person with diabetes has to take insulin. "Did you take your tablets?" became Jim's mantra, glad that they were keeping Mary 'well' and out of hospital. For both of them, that was the big fear factor which meant that Mary never missed a tablet for the next 18 years. But while she was out of hospital, she now had to endure an ever-increasing range of debilitating and dangerous adverse effects of the drugs which in time were to transform her into a piece of psychiatric flotsam - an over-weight, stiff-limbed, kidney-damaged, drooling, tremor-ridden, mind-numbed, middle-aged woman, totally dependent on a resigned and blind Jim.

Then in 1993, a completely fortuitous event marked a turning point in their lives and the beginning of a process of learning, questioning and discovery. With the help of people like Dr. Peter Breggin and Dr. Terry Lynch, of organisations like The Cork Advocacy Network and MindFreedom, Mary began to challenge the orthodox thinking of 'The Medical Model' and with the growing support of Jim and her daughters, began her brave, slow, scary but ultimately empowering journey of liberation from her cocktail of drugs. Discovering the therapeutic benefits of water, music, exercise and relaxation, she started as she says herself "to live again" and make up for all those lost years.

But her story doesn't end there. Angry now with what had happened to her, she and Jim had to overcome the strain this put on their marriage. Finding support among their new friends in the 'alternative treatment' movement, together they embarked on a new phase of their lives. They attended conferences, spoke out on television and in the press and established MindFreedom Ireland. Mary became very active in the 'survivor' movement both nationally and internationally. She is a member of the Board of the European Network of Users and Survivors of Psychiatry, a member of the MindFreedom International Campaign Committee and a member of the International Network of Treatment Alternatives for Recovery. Mary and Jim are also members of Sli Eile (Another Way) the Cork Housing Association for former psychiatric patients, and today, continue their campaign of activism for human rights in the mental health area, specifically in relation to the over-prescription of drugs, forced injections, involuntary detention and the use of electro-convulsive therapy.

Mary and Jim are both teachers. Mary is a music teacher. Jim is a secondary teacher. He worked in Africa for a number of years in the early seventies and has been teaching in Cork for over thirty years.

SOME VOICES FROM THE SURVIVOR MOVEMENT AND ITS ALLIES'

If there were any doubts that we urgently need to hear the voice of the survivor in order to challenge the abuses of the psychiatric system, this book dispels them. Mary's journey through hell contains lessons for us all.'

Lucy Johnstone, Academic Director, Bristol Clinical Psychology Doctorate, Author of 'Users and Abusers of Psychiatry' .

This is a well written splendid case of events. Lots of people and families can identify with Mary's personal experiences. Mary will help and encourage other people thinking of coming off drugs to go ahead and do it. They all will defy psychiatrists and their terrible state control system, get free and live a life free from forced drugging and electro convulsive shocking. Mary has shown the way to recover, she has the courage, willpower and conviction, we share with her. I recommend this book to be read by patients, families and doctors.

Anna de Jonge, Patients Rights Advocate, Hamilton New Zealand

Mary Maddock is a brave and exceptional woman. Soul Survivor chronicles her heroic struggle to overcome not only what initially caused her to become involved in psychiatry, but also what turns out to be the much greater struggle against a psychiatric system that does not allow for recovery, regrowth, resiliency or renewal. By sharing the wisdom she has gained, perhaps others will not have to experience what Mary had to go through.

Jim Gottstein, President/CEO of the Law Project for Psychiatric Rights, Alaska

Soul Survivor is a very apt title for this outstanding autobiography by

Mary Maddock and her husband Jim. Mary not only survives but triumphs over psychiatric tortures of electroshock ("ECT") and forced drugging in some of Ireland's psychoprisons. Thanks to her resistance, spirit and Jim's support, the psychiatrists failed to destroy Mary's mind and soul - they certainly tried. Soul Survivor is an important contribution to the growing psychiatric survivor literature and the antipsychiatry movement for human rights.

Don Weitz Antipsychiatry activist and co-editor of Shrink Resistant: The Struggle against Psychiatry in Canada.

'Thank you Jim and Mary for writing this book. It is thoughtful, eloquent and astute. While very critical of the theories and practices of traditional psychiatry, the book is ultimately a statement of hope. You write that you have been inspired by many different people along your journey, in the end both of you have become an inspiration to others. Thank you.'

Pat Bracken, Clincal Director, West Cork Mental Health Service

I truly and sincerely congratulate you first of as you stand tall as a beacon of light and hope for all of us who have suffered under the hands of psychiatry. Your strength and your personal story really expose what goes on as I can attest as a survivor too. Truly that in Ireland the Empire of psychiatry that is supported by the drug industry will fall with a great crash. As an old colloquialism from North America says: "the bigger they come the harder they fall" and in Ireland the Emperor is now truly "without his clothes". Well done. To be sure!

Nick Vegt, a fellow survivor, New Zealand

Jim and Mary Maddock's outing of Mary's tortuous experience of the Irish medical and psychiatric establishment and its many cohorts, is a uniquely courageous beacon lighted in one of darkest corners of our society. Only relatively few Irish people have blown this whistle and, fewer still if any, gone on, as this couple have, to write their story, found Mind freedom Ireland, and thereafter dedicate many of their waking hours to keep that light in the window.I am honored to call Jim and Mary my friends, and as long as I have breath, am committed to their quest for a medical establishment that foregoes control dressed up as care; care for profit; providing for any citizen who suddenly needs time out, a person-centered, safe, fully resourced healing place of asylum within his own country.

Greg White ,MindFreedom

It is with great pride that I endorse Mary and Jim Maddock. We started on the road to finding our voices together, without knowing each other. Without the courage of Mary our voices might still be silently screaming in the dark. Mary is one of the shining lights that is slowly but inexorably leading us who are mad and proud to a place of equality in society. Jim is a prime example of support, not guardianship. Together they are proof positive of what can be achieved through a love that does not seek to control.

John McCarthy, MindFreedom Ireland

Mary and Jim Maddock's life experiences are described in this wonderful book that unfortunately led Mary to 20 years of incarceration, forced treatment, psychotropic drugs and ECT in psychiatric care in Ireland after the birth of their daughter. The system that was supposed to care for her deprived her of family life and numbed her to despair. After leaving the system against all odds, she went through a marvellous recovery to a life without drugs with Jim's support. I hope that their story will empower others to follow their hard but secured path to recovery free of drugs, or even better, empower them to wellbeing before their lives, unnecessarily, even cross the path of the system itself.

Nuria O'Mahony, Holistic Action Group & Emergency Nurse.

Soul Survivor is the story of Mary Maddock's great escape and redemption from the darkness of a dysfunctional psychiatric regime which almost extinguished her inner light. It bears testimony to the healing powers of the hope, acceptance and support created by her loved ones. It's a story that points to any fault lines running through psychiatry, all of which can be traced to the hideous and erroneous practice of treating problems of living as diseases.

Dr Michael Corry MD, Consultant psychiatrist and psychotherapist. Founder of Depression Dialogues

"Mary Maddock is more than a survivor. She and Jim are trailblazers creating a way out of the mess we have made of psychiatry. Such is our modern professional discomfort with strong human emotion that we have created a whole package of diagnoses, drugs and force to lock it down.

Grief is repackaged as depression, distrust as paranoia, joy as atypical bipolar and concern as Munchausen's by proxy. By recovering, Mary reveals the strength of the human person and the dangers of the powerful coalition of psychiatry and pharmaceuticals. Mary and Jim made and shared their journey at great personal cost. We owe them a debt of gratitude and respect. My hope is that this book finds its way into many homes, wards and clinics so that recovery soon becomes the norm."

Kathy Sinnott, Member of the European Parliament.

DEDICATION

For departed friends Hannelore, Kieran and Stewart, for all those who have suffered and continue to suffer in the psychiatric system and for our two daughters, Claire and Sheena.

Soul Survivor
A Personal Encounter with Psychiatry
Mary & Jim Maddock
with a forward by Dr Terry Lynch

Published by Asylum

29 Heathbank Road, Cheadle Heath, Stockport SK3 0UP

Series editor Terence McLaughlin

Designed by Grania@estrelladesign

Illustration by Daniel Jones

Printed by RAP Spiderweb

Clock Street, Hollinwood, Oldham, OL9 7LY

Distributed by Asylum Associates

Limbrick Centre, Limbrick Road, Sheffield S6 2PE

ISBN 0-9544030-2-7
978-0-9544030-2-7

CONTENTS

Acknowledgements 16

Forward by Terry Lynch 17

Introduction 20

1   Miraculous Football 22

2   Convent Life 25

3   Disillusionment 31

4   Liberation 34

5   Wedding Bells 37

6   Nightmare 44

7   Happy Days 51

8   Déjà vu 57

9   Manic Depressive 63

10   Adverse Effects 67

11   Turning Point 72

12   Overcoming Fear 76

13   Water Wate 82

14   Anger 85

15   Action 89

16   Coming Out 95

17   Danish Delight 102

18   Stop, Stop, Stop 109

19   Darkness and Light 118

20   Hindsight 131

Epilogue 140

Acknowledgements

W e would like to acknowledge with gratitude the help and encouragement of our families and friends. In addition, we would like to thank Grainne Humphrys for permission to reproduce her poem Schizophrenia; John McCarthy for permission to reproduce his poem 'The Head, Dr. Peter Breggin for permission to quote from 'Toxic Psychiatry'; Dr. Terry Lynch for permission to quote from 'Beyond Prozac'; Dr. Lucy Johnstone for permission to quote from 'Users and Abusers of Psychiatry'; Charles Medawar and Professor Anita Hardon for permission to quote from 'Medicines Out of Control?'and Peter Lehmann for permission to quote from 'Coming Off Psychiatric Drugs'. Finally, we would like to express our deep gratitude to Dr Terry McLaughlin and Asylum Publications. It was the result of a fateful meeting with Terry at the INTAR Conference in Killarney in December 2005 that this book eventually saw the light of day.

NOTES TO THE READER

The story is told in two voices. Although it will be clear who is speaking, a change of voice is marked by an extra space.

NOTE ON THE DANGER OF STOPPING DRUGS QUICKLY.

Psychiatric drugs should never be stopped abruptly. The more slowly you withdraw, the fewer bad effects you will suffer. It is recommended that any withdrawing should only be done under informed medical supervision.

Forward

I first met Mary and Jim Maddock in 2001. At that time, my book Beyond Prozac had been published, coinciding with a growing international concern regarding the care of people experiencing mental health problems. Beyond Prozac is in essence an expression of major concern regarding the misguided mental health services approach to mental health problems. As such, my book struck a chord with many users of mental health services. The publication of my book also coincided with Mary Maddock's journey of recovery from many years of psychiatric medication and involvement with the psychiatric mental health services.

Mary first contacted me to offer her support for my expressions of concern about mental health care. I am happy that my book was of some help and support for her and her family as she embarked on the journey of recovery of her Self and her life, of recovery from the mental health services. Since that initial contact, Mary, Jim and I have been in regular contact, contact which has over the years developed into friendship.

Soul Survivor is, above all, a human story. It is the story of Mary's life, of the years of trauma that followed from her contact with the mental health services. Within the pages of this book, there are echoes of the experiences of many people who find themselves attending the mental health services, including not being listened to or feeling respected; the medical obsession with diagnoses rather than understanding the problem and developing a truly therapeutic relationship; with mind-numbing and mood-altering substances (otherwise known as medication) rather than working with the person and their loved ones towards recovery. I do believe that medication has a place, but not to the degree to which it currently dominates mental care.

In recent years, Mary has devoted a great deal of her time to supporting others who find themselves in a similar situation as she found herself in many years ago. Mary brings to this work an effective combination of gentleness, humility, a steely resolve and determination. She is very well informed, and always in the background is her memory of her own personal experiences and those of many people she has come to know over the years.

Mental health service providers owe it to mental health service users to take notice of issues which can be extremely important to the person, but are often dismissed by mental health service providers as being trivial, of little or no importance. Photographs taken during her years on medication are a sharp contrast to how Mary is now; back then, she had gained several stone in weight; her eyes and general demeanour appear 'doped', as if her spirit and being was sedated and numbed. A keen musician, Mary's ability to work with music creatively was seriously diminished while on medication. All of the above have returned since Mary came off medication, much to Mary's delight.

Mary is one of the gentlest people I know. She is also one of the most effective people I know. This book reflects her ability to relate with warmth and love. Her motivation stems from a deep passion regarding how human beings should be treated, with respect and dignity, how precious human life must be fostered and supported, especially at difficult times.

It has also been my pleasure to come to know Jim, Mary's husband. Jim and Mary are a team. Their mutual love and dedication to the well-being of each other is palpable when one is around them. I imagine that Jim's support for Mary, both through the very difficult times described in this book, and in more recent, better times, has been invaluable for Mary. Jim and Mary are quite a team. They both dedicate much of their time to the furthering of the cause of the user of mental health services; towards shifting the focus of mental health care towards recovery, compassion, respect and dignity. I fully support them in this work.

This book has many themes running through it. Not least amongst these themes are the nightmare scenario that can sometimes unfold for a person who comes into contact with the mental health services, how difficult it is to disconnect from these services and the woeful lack of support and respect people receive if they decide, as is their right, to conscientiously disagree with the advice of their doctors. The theme of recovery is also central to the book.

Mary's experience of coming off medication may have been easier than the experience of many others. Reducing or stopping medication is not to be taken lightly. It is a particularly risky endeavour if done without the support and guidance of someone with considerable understanding of the drugs and the risks involved in reducing medication. Many people who have reduced medication have found themselves back in hospital fairly quickly, particularly if they have reduced or stopped the medication rapidly.

Mary's story is a story of recovery of Self. It is a striking story, told with clarity and honesty. This book should be required reading in training courses of psychiatrists, GPs, and all involved in the provision of mental health services. Mental health services providers must develop the maturity to look outside the box of their own particular belief system (discussed in detail in Beyond Prozac) and see the validity of the person's story, their experience. This one change would have a major positive impact on the quality of help and support given to users of the mental health services.

Terry Lynch

Introduction

'Primum Non Nocere - First Do No Harm'. While literally not part of the Hippocratic Oath, the sentiment expressed is nonetheless generally accepted as a basic norm for all those in the medical profession. Young, naïve and trusting as we were thirty years ago, we had full faith in the words and deeds of all doctors. In the structured society of the time, we would never have believed, no more than we would never have believed that clerical abuse existed, that doctors would not always be for your good. And it must be said, indeed of the clerics as well as the doctors, that most of them were and still are.

But in the world of psychiatry, which is what this book is specifically concerned with, it has been our experience that such is not the case. Throughout history, emotionally disturbed people have been demonised by society generally, only to be subject to further barbaric and inhumane 'treatments' in frightening and awful institutions which had the audacity to refer to themselves as 'hospitals'.

Even today, the word 'bedlam' from the 18th century hospital of the same name conjures up a frightening image. The term 'lunatic asylum' used in the 19th century continued to be used well into the 20th century. All readers will be familiar with these grey-stoned or red-bricked fortresses, from 'Our Lady's' in Cork to St. Ita's in Portrane, Dublin which still stand as testimony to a shameful chapter of Irish social and medical history.

It has only been in recent years that the full truth about our terrible Magdalene Launderies has been exposed. It's all very well to speak about the 'standards of the time' but abuse and suffering IS abuse and suffering, no matter when it is perpetrated. That is acknowledged today and leaders of religious orders and indeed the Taoiseach himself have all apologised to the victims.

But there has never been an apology to all those countless, sometimes nameless and forgotten victims of psychiatric abuse who have populated our 'hospitals' down all the years. Why has there been no apology? Is it that the politicians are so ashamed of their abject financial neglect throughout the years that they can't bring themselves to apologise? And what of the medical profession, in particular the psychiatrists themselves? Their defence will be that they do care about their 'patients', that they do their best for them and all 'treatments' are designed to help. Well, from our knowledge of the system, from our reading of its history and from our own fairly recent experiences, we can only say that they are at best misguided, at worst active participants and drivers of a system that has sold its soul to the drug companies and has long departed from those fine words of Hippocrates. Because they are doing harm. Let them listen to the voices of their 'patients'. Let them listen to the voices of a growing number of their professional colleagues who are humble enough to say they have been wrong and brave enough to challenge the established orthodoxy of what today is called bio-psychiatry.

It took over 400 years for the Vatican to apologise to Gallileo for speaking the truth. How long more must the victims of psychiatry have to wait?

1 MIRACULOUS FOOTBALL.

" The real voyage of discovery consists not in seeing new landscapes but in having new eyes"

Marcel Proust.

L ooking back now, we often wonder was there some kind of pre-destination at work.

It was certainly uncanny, if not pre-ordained. And strange the part the Basque Country played in it - the Basque Country, the Virgin Mary and football! Deliberately, we delayed our Spanish holiday in 2002 to be at home for Ireland's three early group matches at the World Cup in Japan. Following the heady drama and nationwide excitement of those days, there was a sense of leaving the party early as we sailed out of Rosslare just an hour after the game against Saudi Arabia. But the consolation was that Ireland would play Spain the following Sunday and to be actually in Spain for that would be an experience to savour.

Arriving in Cherbourg on Wednesday, we now had four days to motor down the west coast of France, sufficient time for leisurely stops in Brittany and the slow-paced Ile d'Oleron with its narrow roads and sleepy, slightly run-down fishing villages, wooden houses and long, dune-fringed beaches. Then it was on south, past Bordeaux and through the 'Landes', the flat, heavily forested, practically deserted area that stretches down to the Basque country and the Spanish border crossing at Hendaye. And that was where the Virgin Mary had come into it.

Mary was still big in the Ireland of the mid-sixties. Just ten years beforehand, in 1954, there had been a special Marian Year as the number of mountain-top crosses, statues and shrines still testify to today. And like Mecca for Muslims, Lourdes was the place to go, as dioscesan pilgrimages from all over Ireland descended on the little town in the Pyrenees. There were no school tours in those days but in 1965, Mary and her friend Martha, had travelled there, the only two girls from her convent school in Sligo to do so. And amazingly, the following year, my friend Barry and myself made the same trip from our school in Wexford, also the only two from the school to do so! When we discovered that, years later, we both thought our paths were destined to cross. Lourdes at the time was a conflicting mixture of the spiritual and the commercial. The night-time torch-lit procession accompanied by the Ave Maria, was a memorable spectacle. Less so were the souvenir shops, bursting with all kinds of tacky Marian goods from plastic statues full of holy water to glass enclosed replicas of the Basilica, complete with the shook-water snow effect! But for me, the highlight of my 'pilgrimage' was the day-trip by bus, down through the mountains, across the border at Hendaye and on to the Basque city of San Sebastian. In 1966, General Franco still held sway in Spain, with a particularly firm thumbhold over San Sebastian. Barry and I were gob-smacked by the magnificent sweep of the beach and promenade, flanked by shining, white hotels and apartments. This was what continental life was about, a million miles from life in Ireland at the time. And then I had seen it, perched on display in the window of a sports shop. The object of my attention was a gleaming white leather football, complete with black hexagonal panels!

In the Ireland of 1966, soccer was still a minority 'foreign game', yet to undergo the explosion of interest following the World Cup participation of the 1990's. It was played in Dublin and a few of the bigger towns on wet, heavy pitches by men with robust, leather boots who kicked equally robust, heavy, leather brown balls. But on the continent, it was different. It was a glamorous, skilful, intelligent and beautiful game and nothing epitomised it more than the beautiful, gleaming, snow-white leather ball and its gleaming, jet-black hexagonal panels which now, more than any torch-lit procession or Ave Marias, provided for me, the spiritual, emotional and imaginative highlight of my pilgrimage! It was love at first sight. I had to buy it even though it made a huge dent in my limited spending money.

And now, thirty-six years later, we were both back in the Basque country and while neither of us had any desire to re-visit Lourdes, football was still very much on the agenda. We drove on past San Sebastian with its golden beaches and windows full of footballs, then turned off the motor-way and took the scenic, winding, narrow road along the Costa Vasca to Lekeitio, a busy Basque fishing port. For the big match on Sunday afternoon, I donned my Ireland tee-shirt and we headed for a bar on the quayside. Expecting a packed house, we were surprised to see so few people inside. The next surprise was when the Spanish National Anthem was played, the sound on the television was turned completely down. This was indeed Euskal Herria - the Basque heartland. By now, there were about twenty half-interested spectators in the bar but all they wanted to see was a Spanish defeat! The Spanish goal after 15 minutes was greeted by a deafening silence. It was weird and not what we had expected. People continued to drift in and out. We were thinking of the atmosphere in pubs all over Ireland. Following the penalty shoot-out and Ireland's exit, we were left with a numb feeling. There was no jubilation on the streets outside, just a few condoling handshakes from locals, seeing the Ireland tee-shirt. Despite the disappointment, we still had two weeks of our holiday ahead of us as we set off the next morning for Bilbao. This was another step back in time for us and another reason why we had decided to spend our holidays there. Mary had spent a summer working as an au pair there in 1973 and the following year, we had returned to the city on our honeymoon. That was just two years after she had left the convent in the west of Ireland where she had spent seven years as a nun.....

Meeting the locals in a Basque bar.

2 CONVENT LIFE

"Our ideals are our better selves"

Amos Alcott.

I was a very lucky person. I had fallen in love with a very special man and I was about to have my first child. There was a time when I had thought I would never, ever have a baby. That was when, for seven years, I had lived as a nun in a convent in the west of Ireland. For most of that time, I was convinced that I would spend the rest of my life there.

When I entered, it was an enclosed order and the regime was very strict. Silence, prayer, work and order were very important. As a boarder for five years beforehand, I had been very impressed by the nuns and their work and at the tender age of 17, I wanted to join them, much to the disgust of my mother. When I decided to tell my family, I had told my father first because I thought he would be more agreeable to the idea.

I will always remember the journey to the convent the day I entered. My father said to me on the way "If you ever want to come back to us again, we will always be there for you." The journey seemed an eternity though it was only about twenty miles. I had very mixed emotions of sadness and excitement as I said farewell to my family before changing out of my favourite top and skirt for the last time and donning a sombre, black dress and a most peculiar hat which were to mark me out as what I had now become - a postulant. Four other girls entered with me at that time. Our surroundings were very dreary and rules and regulations were very important. Our only compensation in life was the good food we were given and the friendship we had together as a group. In the Novitiat altogether, there were about twenty young girls all eager to be good, do the right thing and eventually earn the big reward - Heaven! When I arrived in 1965, the atmosphere was still pre-Vatican 11 so times were very hard.

Every morning we got up before six o'clock, dressed and went to the chapel half asleep to meditate for nearly an hour before Mass. The Mass was in Latin and the more masses you could attend, the better. Sometime we would have three or four one after the other! After that, we would have breakfast in strict silence. The refectory was a very dreary place as we all sat at the middle table looking at each other but never being able to say a word. After breakfast, our big task in life was to keep the convent clean. It was a very big building full of dormitories and classrooms. There was no room for anyone who was afraid of hard labour. One of the jobs we had to do from time to time was to clean The Nun's Chapel. This was a very complicated task because of all the ornamentation in the wooden pews, panels and screens. The dust would lodge in all sorts of places and we were ordered to dust with three different dusters up to three times! It was demanding and physical work but the strong bond we all had with each other kept us going. Then there would be more praying and more silence. Rules and regulations were strictly enforced. The Great Silence was from 8.30 pm until after breakfast the next morning. If you broke any of these rules, you were expected to confess in front of the whole community in the refectory. At every meal, there was a special time when the Reverend Mother would clap her hands and some of the nuns would confess to breaking some rule or other. A major transgression at the time would be for a Novice to speak to a Community nun. Even though we lived in the same house, we could never speak to one another! This rule was designed to prevent what was referred to as 'a particular friendship'.

I'll never forget my first Christmas in the convent. We were told something different and exciting was going to happen. All it turned out to be was that we had some seasonal music in the refectory! When I walked in and heard it, tears welled up in my eyes and I was struck with the pangs of homesickness. All the nuns up to this time had a very old-fashioned habit consisting of a long black dress and a veil that didn't allow vision on either side. There was also a stiff piece of white material in front of the breast called a gamp. There were complaints that eating was very difficult, especially at the beginning until you became used to it. Luckily, before we received the habit, it was decided to introduce a more modern dress. There was great excitement and we were all delighted. I can remember well the first time I saw all the nuns in their new garb. Some of them looked as if they were naked! It must have been very difficult for the older ones.

The second year was called The Spiritual Year and at the beginning, all five of us received The White Veil in a big ceremony attended by my mother, father, two brothers and sister. I wore a white bridal dress which I picked out myself. Not wishing to be vain, I deliberately choose the least attractive dress I could. Of course, the Bishop was present in all his regalia and the ceremony was very long and complicated. We all had many responsible duties to carry out and it was quite a nerve-racking day. There was a huge reception afterwards but after the tension and excitement of the day, none of us had much of a stomach for it.

For the first three months of The Spiritual Year, we never could speak except at recreation time for an hour in the afternoon and again after tea. We were only allowed one visit from our families for the whole year. There was still much hard physical work. Our Novice Mistress had us spend many a day pulling away briars and weeds from a pathway near a house in the grounds of the convent where we spent a lot of time in prayer and study. During this time, we had to write a thesis called 'The Church - the Sacrament of Christ'. I enjoyed this period as we were now beginning to hear about the Second Vatican Council. We read and studied its new documents which I found exciting. There was to be less emphasis on Hierarchy and more on the people of God, there was good to be found in the other churches and a spirit of ecumenism was to prevail. At this time also, some novices from the other four houses of the order in Ireland, joined us. This was exciting too because we were meeting people from other parts of the country and making new friends.

Our Novice Mistress also decided to enrol us for further biblical and theological studies in the Divine Word Mission in Donamon, Co. Roscommon. Donamon was sixty miles away. I had a driver's licence because my father had renewed it every year even though it seemed at the time that it would not be of any use. But now it was to earn me a job as a chauffeur for the trip to Donammon. I had driven very little before I entered the convent so it was decided that my father would give me lessons. I was delighted because I would be able to see him more often and get outside the enclosed walls for a while. After a few lessons, it was decided that I was ready for a long drive to Dublin. One of the professed nuns with a driver's licence came with me. For a long time, I was stuck behind a big lorry and she thought I would never overtake but somehow, we got to Dublin and back! Now I was ready for my weekly drive to Donamon. On this journey, we always passed through a crossroad in my own village. Of course, I could never stop at my own house but my mother was always waiting at the crossroad with sweets and chocolate for the journey. She never missed a day. In the car, the conversation was often very strained as we were in the company of the Novice Mistress and naturally, we prayed on the journey too. She always had her eye on the speedometer so there was no danger of me breaking the speed limit! She was a very good woman but I think she tried to be too good and expected us to be the same.

Donamon was like a breath of fresh air. Open-minded and challenging, I asked many questions and saw how closed the Catholic Church was. It gave me hope and I thought with time, things would change. Being a seminary, we were now also meeting the opposite sex but the watchful eye of the Novice Mistress meant we didn't have time to form any lasting relationships. For the first four years, the Order was still very enclosed but then it was announced that we could have a holiday at home for ten days. You can imagine the excitement when we were told the news. Some of the nuns had not been home for over fifty years. Even if a close family member had died, no one ever attended the funeral!

The young women in the Novitiate were all very talented. We had poets, writers, artists and musicians. For our Novice Mistress's Silver Jubilee, we decided to do something special. I chose to write a piece of music for the piano as this was what I loved with a passion. On another occasion, we decided to do a production of The Mikado. This wasn't very easy as we only had about twenty to choose from. One of the group had always played the principal part in the operas when she had been a student. We spent a long time rehearsing. I was one of the Three Little Maids. We were not allowed to remove our habits so we had to improvise for our costumes. It went down very well, so much so that our Novice Mistress thought we should do a repeat performance the following night for the Bishop, which we considered to be a great honour.

I loved the singing and music that were an integral part of convent life It was one of the things that kept me going all those years. We would practice for hours for mass and especially for important feast days. We always sang in three-part harmony. I sang second soprano. Midnight Mass at Christmas required special preparation. We all only possessed two habits. We would get one ready especially well for that night. When the time came for us to go to the chapel, we all looked cleaner than usual. It was the only time we were allowed to be up so late so everything felt very different. I felt almost in another world. As time went on, we were allowed to speak at meals on special occasions such as Christmas and feast days. We had specially prepared food - even brandy butter at Christmas! Everyone had a feast day. Mine was the 3rd of October, the Feast of St. Therese. I wanted the name 'Therese' because I admired her at the time - mostly because she was young and good looking, not because of her saintly qualities! There was a nun with a similar name at the time and she didn't want me to have the same name so I ended up with Theresina which I felt very lucky to receive. This was to be later shortened to Terry by my close friends.

From time to time, someone would decide to leave the convent. Mostly, no one ever knew beforehand. Just suddenly, that person would be gone and never spoken about again - no such thing as "Goodbye and we'll keep in touch". Very little help was received by anyone to enable them to survive in the world after that. You had to sink or swim. Some of the girls were even shunned by their families and had to put themselves through university working every minute they had.

Then came the time for my First Profession and I took my vows of Chastity, Poverty, Obedience and the Education of Youth. I exchanged my white veil for a black one. This was the beginning of a three year probationary period before the huge ceremony, in the presence of the Bishop, my mother and father, sister and two brothers and the entire community, of my Final Profession. There was a big build-up to the day, with retreats and many preparatory rehearsals for what was quite a nerve-racking occasion, not unlike a marriage ceremony. I now took my vows for life. I was now a fully fledged 'community' nun. As such, I could no longer speak to the other novices and though I could speak to my 'community' sisters, I must confess to some early disillusionment when I realised the very different views and philosophies they held from me. Then I was sent to Athlone on a biology course for three weeks. This was my first taste of some freedom again. It was the time Neil Armstrong walked on the moon for the first time. I had always liked science in school and found the course very interesting. I made friends with two young female teachers from Cork. I was able to visit the local hotel by the lake with them and even go to the cinema, something I hadn't done for years. My parents came to visit often and took me on trips in the area to Clonmacnoise and Birr Castle. I remember this as an especially nice time. When I got back to the convent and reality, I was asked to teach science to the three classes of First Years, a daunting task but one which I warmed to and actually greatly enjoyed at the end.

As a postulant.

3 DISILLUSIONMENT.

"Wisdom comes by disillusionment"

George Santanyana.

Eventually the time came for me to go to College. I was given a choice of studying science or cathecetics. I opted for the latter because I was still so interested in saving the world. I had an initial interview where I was asked some deep philosophical questions which I really enjoyed. The college was The Mater Dei Institute in Dublin. I was to stay in a house belonging to the Order in an exclusive part of the city. I had only been in Dublin a few times as a child. After my enclosed life in the convent, the city seemed a huge place and getting around was almost impossible. But I soon got my bearings and found it all very exciting. It was great to live in a normal house again. Sr. Patricia was in charge of us and although she fed us well, she was very strict and narrow-minded.

By this time I had learned to play the guitar. I had also been awarded a Piano Diploma from the Leinster School of Music and Drama and had taught piano for some years. The relaxation of the regime in the convent meant that I was able to listen to the L.P.s my brother bought into me, including a new duet he had discovered - Simon and Garfunkel and their superb Bridge Over Troubled Water. Mater Dei was on the other side of the city so every morning, I travelled on the No. 11 bus. The newly built college had an exciting, modern feel to it. I studied Theology, Philosophy, Psychology, the Bible and also English and Music. Most of my fellow students were either nuns or brothers but there were also some lay students. Soon, two of them, Denise and Liam, had become my best friends. We spent a lot of time together. This was considered unusual at the time as the religious orders tended to keep to themselves. Music was our big bond. I played all the pop tunes I knew and taught Liam to play the guitar. He was a big Beatles fan and in turn, introduced me to many of their songs which I had missed out on in the convent.

At lectures, I was something of a Devil's Advocate, always asking questions. I read a lot and was very influenced by The Death of God Theology. I was now beginning to become more and more disillusioned with religion and Catholicism in particular. To be a nun was getting more and more difficult. I began to change from the habit into lay clothes on occasions, most memorably a time I visited the Simon Community. I thought the habit was a hindrance. People didn't know who you really were and it stood for a lot of things I was no longer beginning to believe in. I had my sister's black mini-skirt and top and that was all I needed. My hair was long under the veil. I choose the public toilets in O'Connell Street to make the change. As I was going in, there was a woman cleaning the wash-hand basins. I was the only one there so she noticed me on the way in. You can imagine her face a few minutes later when I emerged in my mini-skirt complete with long, red flowing hair! Then it was off to the Simon Community for the first time with my two friends. I can't remember how I got back that night. Sr. Patricia would have dropped dead if she knew! I changed a few more times after that. One time on holidays, I even went to a hotel in Sligo with my sister Josephine and her boyfriend Martin. This was very daring as I could easily have bumped into some of the other nuns. Luckily, I didn't. Leonard Cohen was another favourite of ours at the time. We sang Suzanne, So Long Maryanne and of course, The Sisters of Mercy though I didn't realise who the Sisters of Mercy really were! One of Simon and Garfunkel's - Cathy's Song- began to take on a special significance for me, specially the line "I stand alone without belief".

I was now beginning to question my role in life more and more. What I wanted to do was help change society but being a nun wasn't helping to do this at all. Religious orders and the Catholic Church were not challenging people. They were only helping to maintain the status quo as far as I could see. They were not challenging the rich or doing enough to help the poor. Rules and regulations were still more important. Sex was still the biggest sin. A man could have six houses and six cars but very few priests or nuns would ever criticise him. Many of my sisters of my age were leaving one by one for different reasons. It was like remaining on board a sinking ship. So eventually I made the decision to leave. It didn't take very long. I decided to tell the Reverend Mother. I almost felt she was glad because I think she saw the young nuns as some kind of a disturbance. Having this over was a great relief. The next big task was to visit the Bishop in order to receive dispensation from my four vows - Poverty, Chastity, Obedience and Education of Youth. All the documentation was in Latin. The Bishop translated it very quickly and left me to figure it out as best I could. His attitude was very condescending. His final words to me were "Goodbye my child." This was the same Bishop who had once the idea, when I was in the Novitiate, that we would clean his Palace from top to bottom. After we had completed the task, he presented us with a box of biscuits! Our reward would be 'in heaven' for following a 'poor, humble cross-bearing Christ'. He saw no contradiction in living in a Palace. Another young nun, who left shortly after me, had, on a famous occasion, bravely referred to him as "a pompous bastard" in front of the whole community! How I would have loved to have been there at the time.

I was a happy girl when I joined my mother a few minutes later. She was always there for me. I felt my father was a little disappointed when I had first broken the news to them but my mother was delighted! So after seven years in a habit, I was back in the real world again.

4 LIBERATION.

"Be a lamp unto yourself. Work out your liberation with diligence"

Buddah.

A fter leaving, I got very little support from the convent where I had spent seven years. Once you left, you were very much on your own as far as they were concerned. My mother and father were my strong support. There was always money in the post office for me if I was short. At the same time, the adjustment from the secure life of the convent to the freedom and excitement of the real world was very difficult. What was I to do now?

I decided to go to university and enrolled in U.C.D. to study Maths, Philosophy and Psychology. I moved into a small flat in Rathgar along with two other ex-nuns. It was now late November and college was well under way. This proved a particular handicap when studying Maths. As time went on, college became less and less interesting. The idea of one person lecturing to more than 500 people never inspired me. Philosophy and Psychology were dull and dreary, not the exciting challenge I had expected. By now, I was 24 and would be at least 28 by the time I graduated - an old woman in those days! After a few months, I decided to leave and 'drift' for a while. In hindsight, it was something I needed to do. I had made some new 'hippy' friends at this stage and was attracted by the culture of 'flower power' and its long dresses. I was now buying mine in the Dandelion Green market.

That summer, I decided to go to Spain as an au pair with Denise, my friend from Mater Dei. She had been in Bilbao the previous year and knew the ropes. We set off on the ferry from Dun Laoghaire full of excitement. Arriving in Hollyhead, we decided to hitch to London as we didn't have too much money. Two young girls found it very easy to get lifts and we had no fears in those days. It was a far cry from the enclosed order of a few years earlier to now find myself perched high in the cab of a juggernaut being chatted up by the driver! When we finally arrived in London, we looked up a long lost cousin of mine and stayed with him for the night. The next morning, we caught our student flight to Bilbao. I had no Spanish whatsoever and the family I was working for had no English. I had studied French for the Leaving Cert. and it was some help. I had two young children to look after, Ithor who was two and Irache who was one. I had never looked after children so young before so I found this a very difficult task compounded by the fact I was in a foreign country where I couldn't speak the language. In such circumstances, I can tell you, I soon picked it up! The family lived in Neguri, a suburb of Bilbao in one of the many apartment blocks which were a feature of the city. This was all new to me as there were very few in Ireland at that time. I was kept very busy with the children. We would go to the park every day. This was very necessary having no garden. I also took them to the beach. One day Ithor hurt his ankle and couldn't walk home. It was more than a mile back and all uphill. I had to put him in the buggy and carry Irache in my arms all the way home in the sweltering heat and then climb the stairs to the fourth floor as there was no lift in the block! On another occasion, I took the tram to visit a friend and on the way home stopped off at a tavern called La Pianola. I thought some other friends of mine would be there and they would walk me home the last two miles to the apartment but to my surprise, the tavern was closed that night as it was Monday. The last tram had gone so I had to walk home along a dark and lonely road by myself. It was a scary experience especially when a car drove past me a few times in a very suspicious manner. Fortunately, I just reached home at that stage but the perspiration was running down my back as I finally gained the sanctuary of the apartment.

I had just one day off every week when we would go into Bilbao. It was very exciting being in a big city other than Dublin. We would visit the small and friendly tapas bars, sample the red wine which was very cheap and feast on the delicious sea-food snacks and other exotic delicacies which were to be found on every counter. It was the custom of the locals to go from bar to bar so we followed suit no problem. At the end of the night we would visit Flask, the trendiest disco in town. I was only used to dance-halls in Ireland and a few not too sophisticated discos in Dublin but Flask was a young girl's dream for dancing. I was carried away by the rhythm, the lights and the atmosphere and could have stayed dancing all night. I was referred to as a 'woppa' because of my fair complexion and long auburn hair. I had no trouble getting boyfriends and of course had to make up for all that lost time in the convent!

When our time in Neguri was finished, we decided to hitch-hike to Madrid and from there we hoped to go to Ibiza, which then was something of a Mecca for hippies. It was a great feeling of liberation after minding the children for all the summer. By that stage, I could speak and understand Spanish quite well and put it to practice on the various lifts we got. Then disaster struck. Racing to a car that had stopped for us outside of Valladolid, we left one of my bags behind on the roadside and didn't realize it until we had gone nearly a hundred miles. It was the bag which contained my passport, student's card, camera and most importantly, the money which I had saved from my summer's work. Very kindly, the man in the car drove all the way back to the spot but of course the bag was gone. We checked at the Guarda Civilia station but it was no good. Eventually in Madrid, we found the Irish Embassy and they arranged a new passport for me which enabled me to get another student card, without which I would not have been able to get the cheap flight back to London. The Embassy told me I could receive money from home but I was too proud to do that. I was really very foolish as my mother was always so generous to me and would never have seen me stuck. Our plans for Ibiza had to be abandoned and we returned to Bilbao where fortunately, I had left a little money, which, along with a loan from my friend, was just enough to get me back to London. I had to look up my cousin again and he gave me the fiver I needed to get the train to Hollyhead and the ferry back to Ireland. On the way, presumably because of my hippy attire, I was actually asked for my passport but I finally landed safely and was met by my parents, who drove me home to Sligo.

With my friend Loretta

5 WEDDING BELLS.

"To love someone deeply give you strength. Being loved by someone deeply gives you courage"

LeoTzu.

It was now September, 1973. For a one-time hippy, I now took a more conventional direction and enrolled for a commercial course in Ballaghdereen. In the evenings, I helped out in my brother Paddy's pub, met the local lads and went dancing as often as I could.

In December, I visited my sister who was teaching in the Mercy Convent in Belmullet. The staff were having a party in the local pub and I was invited along. It was a night that was to change my life as it was the night I first met the man I was destined to marry. Jim was also a teacher on the staff. At first glance, I thought he was tall and handsome and as we got talking, I found him very interesting. What was a man from Wexford doing in the wilds of Mayo, at the other end of the country? Was this what destiny was about? To me, Wexford was just a place on the map, a place I had never visited. We got on very well that night and though we had a lot in common, I didn't really expect anything more to come of it. Then one day in the Spring, he turned up out of the blue when my sister answered a knock on the door. I couldn't believe it when he walked in! I had glasses on watching television and whipped them off as fast as I could. He afterwards told me it was a flash of thigh exposed by my mini-skirt that first caught his eye! We adjourned to the pub with with my sister Josephine and her boyfriend Martin and even though it was only my second time meeting him, already I was feeling like I had known him a long time.

He had been teaching in Africa for three years where he had travelled widely. On his way home, he had journeyed around India and much of Europe. Not quite a hippy but with an adventurous spirit, we had a lot of ideals in common. He wasn't too interested in money or possessions. After that, we began to meet at weekends. That Easter, the weather was cold but dry and sunny. We spent a few days in Dublin, listened to music in The Stag's Head, had another lovely day in Glendalough before driving to Rosslare where I met his parents for the first time. We also travelled to Cork to visit another ex-nun friend of mine and found ourselves falling in love with the city as well as with each other. Soon we were talking about getting married, something I had never thought I would do, especially so soon. Jim changed my mind completely. It all seemed like a natural progression.

Certainly, it was a whirl-wind romance. I hadn't believed it at first when Mary told me she had been a nun but I was attracted by her free spirit and the accounts of her somewhat hippy life-style she had lived after leaving. We didn't become engaged but announced to all that we would marry the following August. I handed in my notice in Belmullet and didn't even look for another job elsewhere in the country. Instead, in our adventurous and impractical way, we planned to return to Spain where we thought we could live, Mary teaching music, me English. So we had married on the August Bank Holiday Monday in the U.C.D. chapel in Belfield.

Our respective parents had only met for the first time the previous evening. If there were any doubts or reservations about the speed of events, none was expressed. Mary's sister Josephine had married Martin just three weeks previously but had chosen to do so in Rome. For their remaining daughter, Mary's parents intended to have a day out. The reception was held in Killiney Castle but without the glitz of limousines or champagne receptions. Mary wore a beige cotton dress bought in her favourite Dandelion Green shop. Her floral bouquet was a single red rose, plucked in the hotel garden on her way to the church in her brother Tommy's car. They had got a puncture which meant a later than usual arrival but apart from that, everything went well. Sister Kevin, Mary's old music teacher, played the organ and led the prayers.

There was little by way of protocol or formality, a few short speeches and that was it. But everybody enjoyed themselves. They drank, ate, sang and danced, threw the bride in the air , threw the groom in the air, threw our car (a mini) in the air before we set off on what was the first leg of our honeymoon down to Rosslare, where we would spend a few days before leaving on the ferry. The plan was to combine our honeymoon with a reconnaissance trip to Spain where we hoped to arrange our jobs and accommodation. But we were not going to drive to Spain, we were going to hitch-hike! It was to be a romantic if not the most luxurious of honeymoons. With our rucksacks on our backs, we boarded the ferry Caledonian Princess for Fishguard. On the voyage we were treated to lunch in the First Class restaurant by friends of mine who worked on the ferry. Labouring up the steep hill of Fishguard's main street, we stopped for a drink in The Royal Oak before chancing our luck just outside the town. Our destination was Southampton where we would catch a ferry to Santander. Our first lift brought us 15 miles to Haverford West. From our previous experiences, we both considered ourselves seasoned hitch-hikers. It was still always an adventure with its total unpredictability, not knowing who we were going to meet, how far we were going to travel, or where we were going to sleep, a not unimportant consideration on a honeymoon!

This was borne out with our next two lifts. The first was of a mere 6 miles but that was followed by an amazing trip all the way across south Wales, across the Severn Bridge and on to Stowe, a picturesque town in the Cotswolds. Our benefactor was a Mr. Hanks, driving a high-powered Rover who, having driven around town in a vain attempt to secure accommodation, offered us the use of a caravan in the grounds of his own home, complete with full English breakfast the next morning. At noon the following day, we found ourselves at a roundabout in Abbingdon, just south of Oxford. From there we got a lift in an articulated truck which brought us all the way to the docks in Southampton. The next ferry to Spain was not until the following evening so we booked into a newly-opened, delightful Tudor-style guesthouse and that night went to see the film version of the hippy musical 'Hair'. The next day we strolled around town and were invited to join a Sikh wedding celebration we stumbled upon in The Duke of Wellington, the oldest tavern in town. We sailed out of Southampton on the Monte Toledo on Friday evening at seven o'clock and were due in Santander at seven o'clock the following Sunday morning.

At the beginning, the voyage was very smooth. Sailing down the Solent, past Cowes and out into the English Channel past The Needles, we treated ourselves to dinner, again in the First Class restaurant and danced to a late hour before retiring to squeeze into a single bunk in our two-berth cabin! After all, we were on our 'Luna de Miela' as Mary explained to the Spanish steward. The Bay of Biscay can experience severe summer storms and it was our misfortune to run into a Force 10 the next day. Mary woke up feeling sick. This is not morning sickness, you can't be pregnant yet, we joked. But she spent most of the day in her bunk while I entertained myself by watching a few stalwart passengers engage in some clay-pigeon shooting from the stern, despite the incredible rough and rocking conditions. The storm abated during the night and we berthed in Santander on Sunday morning, just an hour behind schedule.

Long hair, beards and rucksacks were not too common in Santander in 1974. As in 1966, General Franco still held sway over a predominately Catholic and conservative Spain. So a tiring search for accommodation around the city centre met with suspicious looks and blank refusals. Being August and peak holiday season may also have been a reason but we sensed an unwelcome mood wherever we went, being stared at as if we were subversive agitators. Mary decided to ring Yone in Bilbao, a hair-dresser friend she had made the previous summer and explain our predicament. Yone told us to come to Bilbao and she would arrange a place for us to stay. With a sense of relief, we boarded a train and sang our full repetoire of Beatle's songs as we reclined on the wooden seats all the way along the coast of Cantabria, through the nostalgically named Laredo and on to the Estacion de Abando just across the river from the Casa Viejo or Old Town in central Bilbao. Yone lived there and she now set about securing accommodation. This proved to be a most difficult undertaking, involving visits to several apartments in the vicinity, protracted and even heated exchanges all in Spanish before eventually a room was acquired. But what an ordeal. Combined with our earlier experience in Santander and her sea-sick voyage, it was all too much for Mary, who tearfully expressed a desire to no longer stay in Spain but instead, return to live in Ireland! It had all been a bit of a hair-brained plan anyway and , though surprised at its timing, given that we were only in the country for less than a day, I tended to concur.

A degree of urgency now entered the situation as it was mid-August and schools in Ireland would reopen in September. Finding a job would be difficult if not impossible. So it was agreed that we spend just a few more days in Bilbao before heading home again. With that definite plan, we intended to enjoy ourselves in the mean time. Mary was eager to show me her haunts from the previous summer. We visited lots of 'tapas' bars including La Pianola and her favourite disco-bar, Flask. Yone and her boyfriend showed us around and we went swimming on the lovely beach at Plentzia, where we were reprimanded by Franco's police for crossing the beach-front road in our swimming gear. We were photographed by a random passer-by in the Old Town, bemused by our appearance. We went shopping in El Gorte Ingles and bought presents for everybody at home. We had a great time by day and it con- tinued by night when we returned to our room with its old iron bed in our apart- ment on the Calle Santa Maria, where the bells from the Cathedral de Santiago wafted gently in through the faded wooden shutters of our balcony window.

We also contacted Elvira and Miguel, the couple for whom Mary had worked the previous summer and spent a few more nights with them in their small, fourth floor apartment, the stairs of which was still fresh in Mary's mind. Because the ferry from Santander was not due to sail until the following Sunday, we decided we would hitch back up through France and catch a ferry from Le Havre back to Rosslare. Miguel and Elvira offered to drive us as far as the French border, stopping en route in San Sebastian for a stroll along the magnificent sweep of the Pasco de la Concha and around the narrow streets of the Zona Romantica where I had fallen in love with a football what seemed like ages ago but in fact was only eight years previously. At Irun, the Spanish border town, we bade farewell to Miguel and Elvira and walked across the border to Hendaye. Still only late afternoon, we tried hitching for a while but without success. Fortunately, there was an old run-down hotel close by, cream- coloured with dark red shutters. We were shown to our room with an ancient wooden bed by an equally ancient, wrinkled and stooped woman. The next morning we had breakfast of coffee and croissants in a shaded little courtyard at the rear, carrying memories as we left of a charming and memorable stay in a place so initially un- attractive. It was a fitting end to our Basque honeymoon. As we climbed the hill out of Hendaye, we had a long road back to Ireland ahead of us and little did we know it, we had an even longer and far more arduous journey ahead of us on the road we call life

Even in 1974, finding a job as a teacher in Ireland was difficult, trying to find one in late August well nigh impossible. But with the boundless optimism of youth, we decided to head for Cork. Neither of us wanted to return to Dublin, we did want to live in a city so it was either Cork or Galway and given our earlier pleasant associat- ions with Cork, Cork it was. We made our base in Cobh and knocked on the door of every school in the city. It so happened that at Douglas Community School, there were two late vacancies. I immediately completed the application forms. Interviews would take place the following week. In the meantime, we also called to schools in Crosshaven, Kinsale, Bandon and Midleton, all to no avail. On the way back to Rosslare, we made further calls in Youghal, Dungarvan and Waterford, the situation at this stage becoming more and more desperate. But it was the same story every- where - a friendly reception, leave your details but nothing doing this year. Our last chance was the interview for Douglas the following Friday morning. We drove back down to Cork the evening before. I had done as much preparation as possible in the meantime. As a complete stranger entering what can be a tightly-knit comm- unity in Cork, I wasn't too hopeful. The comments of a fellow applicant, familiar with the realities of the Cork scene, only served to confirm my pessimism. However, I felt I did a good interview but was it good enough to be one of the two successful applicants out of the hundreds who had originally applied? The following evening I got a phone-call back in Rosslare. It was the Principal of the school, Sean Phelan. I had got the job and would be starting the following Tuesday. We couldn't believe it!

Our run of good luck continued when we arrived in Cork on Monday. Picking up an Evening Echo at the traffic lights on the way in, we noted a flat for rent in Douglas. As it turned out, it was right beside the school and we quickly agreed terms with the landlady, Mrs. Fagan. The school was beginning its first year as a new Community School, having been previously run by the Presentation Brothers. It was an exciting time in Irish education. Altogether, there were twelve new members of staff that September, all young and enthusiastic. In the meantime, Mary advertised for piano lessons and received a good response, travelling around to her pupils' homes in the afternoons.

Life was good. We had a little bit of money, a place of our own, a television with one channel- all that was available in Cork at the time- and each other. We went to the Everyman Theatre, the cinema and the South County pub. We had friends come to visit at weekends and we explored the beauty of East Cork, West Cork and Kerry. The following spring, we decided to buy a house and moved into a three-bedroomed semi in Donnybrook with few of the material comforts so prevalent today. And then in April, Mary found herself pregnant. We were delighted. I remember a warm, sunny, Sunday afternoon having a picnic on the cliffs overlooking the sea at Robertscove. Not even Ireland's shock defeat at the hands of Switzerland in the European Nations Cup that same day seemed to matter.

On my wedding day with my niece, Leta.

6 NIGHTMARE.

"Madness may not be all breakdown. It may also be breakthrough"

R.D.Laing.

After eight months of married life, I found myself pregnant. Jim and I were very excited and didn't care if it was a boy or a girl. We had bought a house near Douglas village and Jim now painted a lovely mural on the wall of what would be the nursery. I had a very difficult pregnancy and felt sick for most of the time. Even though I attended my doctor regularly, I was anaemic and very weak. Along with my gynacologist, we decided to have the baby in St. Finbarr's Hospital. We were told if anything went wrong, this was the best place to be. I wanted Jim to be present and St. Finbarr's was also the only hospital which at that time allowed it. I had never been in hospital before so everything seemed very strange to me. It was very impersonal and matter-of-fact. My labour was long and difficult so I took the gas that was provided for some relief. Jim was by my side throughout. We both noticed that the gas was changing my mood. After a long, long night of hard labour, our daughter Claire was born but I can't remember the moment at all. Luckily, Jim was able to describe it to me later.

The morning of Tuesday, January 27th, 1976 was bright and beautiful. The sky was a cloudless blue, the sun shone, a crisp white frost covered everything and at 10.50 am, our bright and beautiful daughter Claire was born. We had gone to the hospital at seven o'clock the evening before and Mary had gone into a long and arduous labour during which she was given a gas which was meant to afford her some relief. It was after that I noticed her beginning to say some strange, unreal things about dying. I was concerned but not unduly so, thinking it was part of the difficult labour she was experiencing. The nurses too didn't seem concerned. The long labour concluded with the equivalent of a forceps delivery the next morning, a small vacuum-suction cap technique being used instead. I can still see the small raised, circular bump it left on Claire's head, though I was assured it would soon subside. Claire emerged into the world, and weighed in at seven pounds. She stretched her arms and legs and began to cry before being taken away to be checked and cleaned. She was then wrapped in a green sheet and returned to Mary. I doubt she appreciated her presence, given her exhausted state. After that we left the delivery room, Mary to recover from her ordeal while I went home to ring our families with the good news. As chance had it, the first person I met was a neighbour who was a deaf and unable to speak but could use sign language. I stopped the car and excitedly wrote out the news on the frosty side window. As the song said, I felt it really was the dawning of the Age of Aquarius!

The next few days are a bit of a blur. I do remember my parents arriving from Wexford that afternoon and Mary's mother arrived from Sligo with Josephine and Martin. Mary was still very exhausted though I don't recall any of us being overly concerned about her condition. In good spirits, I remember all of us having a celebratory drink in The Briar Rose. But on Thursday, things changed. Mary became very animated and excitable, saying things completely out of character. She was also breast-feeding Claire. That afternoon I had to drive to Ennis with her mother where we would be met by her brother Tommy, who had driven down from Sligo.

In contrast to the lovely weather of the previous Tuesday, there now descended on the country a storm of horrific proportions - howling winds and torrential rain which made for an arduous trip back to Cork. Arriving in the city, I went straight to St. Finbarr's. Matters had worsened in the meantime. Mary was in a very agitated state and I was told - I don't recall being asked - that it would be best for her and the other mothers on the maternity ward if she were transferred to St. Stephen's Hospital at Sarsfield Court, a psychiatric hospital a few miles outside Cork! What followed in the next few hours, I'll never forget. It was like some terrible, frightening, weird dream except that it was no dream. At about ten o'clock that night, against the backdrop of the still raging storm, Mary was put into the back of an ambulance, still in her night clothes. I went along with her while my father and mother followed in their car. Claire was left behind with the nurses in St. Finbarr's. I can't recall if its lights were flashing but the ambulance was driven at what seemed like breakneck speed east along the dual carriageway at Tivoli, around the roundabout at Lota, through the winding street of Glanmire, then off what was then the main road to Dublin and in through the gates of Sarsfield Court.

The hospital had originally been built as a T.B. sanatorium in the 1950's and its airy position in the hills outside Cork had been deliberately chosen. I had often noticed it in passing from the main road but had always thought it was an hotel! I had little knowledge of any kind of hospital in those days, let alone psychiatric hospitals. They were 'mad houses', frightening, forbidding places behind high walls that you stayed as far away from as possible. If you did think of the poor, locked-up inmates, it was more often than not, to make jokes at their expense in a cruel and ignorant manner. Like the orphanages, Magdalen Homes and industrial schools of mid-twentieth century Ireland, mental hospitals were another aspect of Irish life that was swept under the carpet.

As the ambulance sped up the tree-lined avenue of Sarsfield Court that stormy night, its very isolation added to the whole nightmarish experience. Surrounding the four storey hospital building are a number of ground-level units or blocks and the ambulance stopped at the entrance to Unit Four. The rain lashed down as we were bustled inside, down a corridor and into an office. Again, I don't recall being asked to sign any papers but if I was, I'm sure I did on the basis that, even though I didn't like all that was happening, it was something that had to be done for the good of Mary. We were then led to a ward where she was put into a bed and given an injection to sedate her. My father and mother went home but I decided to stay the night, dozing in a chair beside the bed, exhausted after a harrowing day.

The next morning the reality of the surroundings hit home. The patients, male and female, shuffled up and down the long corridor or sat around the Day Room all in a very drugged state. Given the climate in those days, I was taken aback by a patient who introduced himself as a homosexual. My father picked me up and as we drove home that morning, I was glad to leave the place, even as I was shattered to think that Mary, my wife and Claire's mother, was still left behind there.

The best description for the eight weeks I spent in Sarsfield Court is HELL. This was a mental hospital with all the associated connotations. Jim would tell me it was a Psychiatric hospital, not a mental hospital but there was no disguising the fact. At the time, I had no idea whatsoever of psychiatry and all it is about. I didn't know the name of one psychiatric drug apart from Valium and Librium and I knew nothing at all of any side effects. As a result, I was not able to differentiate between what I accepted at the time to be my illness and what might have been drug side effects, which, I now know, can often be mistakenly taken as being part of the diagnosed condition. I was given large doses of Largactil, sometimes in liquid form to act even faster. I can still remember its taste to this day. It was terrible but the effects were even worse. You felt like a zombie. Movement was very slow and I found it almost impossible to concentrate on anything. Consequently, every day was very long and boring with nothing to do except sit around. Jim brought me a jigsaw puzzle which normally I would have found enjoyable but it was almost impossible for me and it was completed by one of the male nurses who spent his days making it instead of attending to his patients. I was very unhappy in the hospital and on one occasion, tried to run away. Medication was the big thing. The whole day was wound around it. Giving it out after meals and again before bedtime seemed to be the nurses main occupation apart from making beds and serving meals and sometimes assaulting patients who were upset. This would take the form of forced injections, something I was often subjected to myself.

I was diagnosed as having Puerperal Psychosis, a severe form of post-natal depression. In addition to drugs, I was also given electric shock treatment. This was and still is used as a treatment on the basis that people with epilepsy don't get depressed. Imagine giving someone a fit and thinking it is going to have good results! I was given eight sessions of shock treatment After each session, I was left with a massive headache and a lot of events were completely wiped out of my memory. This is why I can't remember holding Claire in my arms for the first time. It breaks my heart. She remained in St. Finbarr's for all of this time apart from a few short visits when Jim would bring her out to me. I was missing out on those vital early weeks of bonding with her which was very frustrating. The nurses in St. Finbarr's were very good to her and did everything they could.

Mary was kept in Sarsfield Court for eight weeks, every day of which I went to visit her. At that time, I had an implicit trust in doctors, the medical profession and by extension, psychiatrists. I took it they knew what they were doing and would make Mary better. Any medication prescribed could only be for her benefit. I knew nothing at all of side effects nor were they ever discussed. I was told about post- natal depression and that Mary had an even worse condition called puerperal psychosis. I wasn't too bothered with names. To me, Mary was still Mary. I spoke to her every day. She always appeared sane to me. She played the guitar in the Day Room and we played table-tennis. Certainly, she was restless and at times, weepy, especially saying goodbye to Claire after her visits. But I was told she was not well enough to be discharged. Again, I don't recall any big discussion on the question of E.C.T but again, in my ignorance and naivety, must have gone along with it when suggested by the 'experts'. Sometime in March, Claire was christened in the chapel of St. Finbarr's. Mary was allowed out and her parents and mine were also present. A photograph shows her with Claire in her arms. Mary appears exhausted and her eyes heavy-lidded, the results of her treatment of the previous six weeks. Eventually in April, she was discharged though still on heavy medication.

After eight weeks, it was decided I was ready to go back to society even though, because of all the so-called 'good' treatment I had received, I was now hyperactive and could hardly sit down for any length of time. This was one of the worst experiences I have ever suffered. That Easter, we drove up to Tuam to see Claire, who was now being looked after by Josephine and Martin. We can never thank them enough for that. They had no children of their own at the time and taking on a new baby of just a few weeks must have been very daunting for them. Jim and I went to Donegal for a few days. We thought the break would be good for me but I couldn't enjoy it or relax at all, so restless was I and always wanting to be on the move. On the way back, I visited my friend Sister Kevin in Sligo who suggested we try St. Patrick's Hospital in Dublin. We went to see a G.P. in Ballymote and he furnished us with a letter for St. Pat's.

To her family and me that Easter, Mary still wasn't her usual self and she knew it herself. At the time, we were totally unaware that the restlessness she was experiencing was a recognised side effect of the medication she was taking. To us all, she still wasn't better so we decided to try St. Pat's.

On Easter Monday we drove to Dublin. Strangely, despite her restlessness, Mary was always at ease driving in the car. It was a somewhat unorthodox admission. As far as I can recall, there had been no prior contact with the hospital. All I had was a letter from the G.P. In contrast to the previous experience of Sarsfield Court, as we parked the car under the trees outside the main entrance, St. Pat's looked an altogether more pleasant place. This impression continued as we reported to Reception and were shown into a lovely wood-panelled room with antique furniture and old paintings. Here Mary was assessed by a doctor, who, at one stage , asked her to explain certain well known proverbs which she did without difficulty. In fairness, it was agreed to admit her despite the lack of any previous consultation. But a different picture emerged as a nurse led us to the Admission Ward. The first thing that struck me were the bunches of keys and the locked doors. We were led through one door and up a spiral, iron staircase. This was like a prison!. At the top, there were more locked doors and more again as we walked down a corridor past flimsy, dark wooden cubicles. We then came into an open ward where Mary was given a bed close to the nurses' station. The overall impression was of a crowded school dormitory but I'll never forget the rattle of the keys and the locked doors. Alone, back out in the car a half an hour later, I buried my face in tears.

In Dublin, I longed for Claire every day and was also now separated from Jim, though he came to see me every weekend. I was put on very strong drugs to calm me down and I slept and slept for a few days. When I finally realised where I was, I found myself in a big ward with locked doors, full of people who were all very disturbed. The place was very scary and strange. Now, I was still hyperactive but had to stay in bed all the time, the last thing I wanted to do! This was always the regime in mental hospitals. You had to stay in bed at the beginning no matter what frame of mind you were in. I even wanted to hoover the floor for the want of something to do. This was another world, a world nobody would want to visit, a living nightmare of rattling keys and locked doors. Living in an enclosed order of nuns was nothing by comparison. Eventually, I was considered well enough to leave that awful Admission Ward and was granted a little more freedom. Jim and I wrote to each other every day. Jim kept all my letters. I read them all again many years later and cried bitter tears. You couldn't wear your clothes for the first few weeks. In one letter I wrote "It is Monday morning now and I am waiting to find out if I can put my clothes on or not. I really hope I can." It was a robbing of your dignity. In another letter I wrote "I find the time very long. If I had Claire, she would keep me occupied but I mustn't rush things. I must be brave and fight with all I've got for you and Claire." Even though I was a rebel at heart, I had completely succumbed to the system. The drugs had been very effective in breaking my spirit. Another time I wrote to Jim "I am sorry I was so depressed when you were going but I couldn't help it. I love you so much" and quoted Kahil Gilbrain "That which is our greatest joy is also our greatest sorrow". I was in St. Pat's for eight weeks.

After the Admission Ward, Mary was given a room on the ground floor. This was the better side of St. Pat's. There was good occupational therapy - painting, music, dancing, exercise and walks in the nice garden. There were interesting lectures on Jonathan Swift, the founder and the history of the hospital. Mary was allowed out on visits to the city and eventually, at the end of May, she was discharged. At long last, after four harrowing months, we were re-united with Claire and looking forward to happier times as a family back in Cork.

With our parents at Claire's christening.

7 HAPPY DAYS.

"Learn from yesterday, live for today, hope for tomorrow. The important thing is not to stop questioning"

Einstein.

Being a new mother is never an easy job but I now had summer holidays from school and could help out with the joys of nappy changing in those pre-disposable days! Claire prospered and grew and smiled at everyone in sight. In August, we left her with my parents in Rosslare as we took a motoring holiday in England, re-tracing some of the steps of our hitch-hiking honeymoon of 1974. We called to see Mr. Hanks in Stowe, spent a few days in London and toured what that summer of 1976 was the sunbaked Wessex countryside of Thomas Hardy. We swam on the pebble beach beneath the red cliffs at Sidmouth before driving back across the Severn Bridge to Fishguard, eager to be re-united with Claire.

Life was getting back on an even keel. In September, we both returned to work. Mary taught piano for a few hours in the afternoon when I returned from school to look after Claire. We went through the usual phases with her - teething, injections croup, little mis-haps like the time she fell out of her buggy, her first birthday, her first steps and so on. Mary had been on medication after leaving hospital but was now weaning herself off.

After the first year I was off all drugs and attending no psychiatrist so my true personality returned again. This was a very productive time in my life even though I was very isolated living in a big Cork city suburb without any family and few friends. I joined the local Ladies Club and got to know more people through the socials and other activities we organized. I became chairperson of the club and to contribute something to the community, I also took the children of the estate for singing every weekend, first in our house and later in the local I.C.A. hall. We staged a production of Grease to a packed audience in Ringaskiddy Hall. John Travolta's part was played by teenager Michael McCarthy, who subsequently went on to study music and drama, eventually ending up in London's West End where he played the role of Javere in the hit musical 'Les Miserables; as well as touring with the show in America, Australia and the Far East. I am glad to say he is still the same as ever and has not forgotten his humble origins in the hall of Ringaskiddy.

In the summers we went on holidays, though with money scarce, they tended to be short. In 1977, we went to Paris for a few days, availing of a cheap fare on the ferry from Rosslare to Le Havre, but with no cabins for the 22 hour crossing! We had free accommodation with the parents of the French wife of a colleague at school, who looked after us very well. The following summer we managed a few days in Swansea and in 1979, we toured Kerry and Clare for a week with my parents. That was the first time we had taken Claire with us on holiday. She was now three and enjoying all the attention from her doting grand-parents.

At this stage, we were thinking of a brother or sister for her but the advice was that a second pregnancy would carry a high risk of a second breakdown. It was a time when the issue of contraception was an emotive one in Ireland and we had to avail of Mr. Haughey's 'Irish solution to an Irish problem' and present a doctor's prescription to our local pharmacy to acquire the pill for Mary. So we began to think about adoption and to make enquiries. Following advice from another colleague at work who had been through the process, we decided to apply to St. Patrick's Society in Dublin. We were then put through a long and vigorous procedure of interviews and visits from nuns and social workers before we were told we were accepted and would be placed on a waiting list. Given our history, we were very lucky to be accepted and even with the value of hindsight today, we hope that Sheena feels the same way. We think she does.

Sheena was born on the 4th of January, 1980. On the afternoon of Thursday, March 13th, we received a phone call to say that there was a little baby girl, 10 weeks old ready to join our family and could we be in Dublin to receive her the following Saturday. I was over the moon. I went around to tell all my friends and neighbours in the estate. With no mobile phones, I couldn't tell Jim until he arrived home from training the school soccer team at 6 o'clock. We were all so excited, none more so than Claire, who was going to have a new baby sister! It was now a mad rush to get ready for Dublin. On Friday morning, we descended on the baby department in Roches Stores and bought all the bits and pieces required for a new baby, as until then, we hadn't known whether we would have a boy of a girl. Brimming with excitement, we drove to Dublin where we stayed with Jim's brother John and his wife Catherine, in Portmarnock. On Saturday morning, we drove across the city to Blackrock. Unlike my first encounter with Claire, I can remember that day very vividly and clearly. We were met by Sister Angela who showed us into a large, richly furnished room. We were then left on our own for a few minutes. Outside, the yellow daffodils danced in the March sunshine. Then Sister Angela returned carrying a tiny yellow bundle in her arms. This was Sheena. She looked beautiful and never made a sound all that time when Sister Angela handed her over to me. She was very small as she was only five pounds when she was born, some of the little information we were given. We all took turns in holding her. It was an unforgettable moment. Before Thursday, we hadn't seriously thought about names. That night, after the phonecall, we had scoured the list at the back of our Chambers dictionary and had come across Sheena, the Scottish version of the Gaelic Sinead. Seeing her in her yellow baby-gro looking up at us with her blue eyes, the name sounded just fine.

There was another side to this happy scene of course, one which, though we were aware of it, somehow at the time, we feel we didn't fully appreciate. That was what must have been the most terrible and heart-rending experience of Sheena's mother who, only weeks or maybe even days earlier, had been parted from her own baby daughter, her own flesh and blood. How cruel life could be and yet we were a part of the process. What pain, sorrow, heartbreak and fear she must have endured. Twenty-one long years later, there was to be a happy re-union but at the time, she wasn't to know that. We drove back to Portmarnock with Sheena asleep in my arms in the back of the car. Again, there was great excitement among her new aunt and uncle and cousins, Niall, Fergal and Fiona. Later she fell asleep again only to be woken crying from a roar from her Uncle John, carried away with the excitement of Ireland scoring a try against Wales in that afternoon's Five Nations encounter.

Back in Cork, we got on with our lives now centered around our new ten week old arrival. Both emotionally and physically, Mary felt better prepared for her new role. There was also much more support from friends and neighbours than in Claire's time. and Claire herself, as the big sister, was always pleased to help out. Nevertheless, we still had an anxious wait with Sheena before the final Adoption Order would be signed. In theory, there was still the possibility of some snag arising and of Sheena being taken from us. Eventually, after an eight month wait, all was in order and we were all called before a meeting of the Adoption Board in Cork where all the formalities were legally finalised. Now we could proceed with an official christening ceremony which we arranged for the Sunday after Christmas in the church in Frankfield. The ceremony was to be conducted by Fr. Dave McAuliffe, the local curate renowned for his unorthodox style. An hour beforehand, Fr. Dave arrived at our house. He had an idea. As it was the Feast of the Holy Family, he thought he would conduct the christening in the middle of the twelve o'clock mass, instead of delivering his usual sermon! So from our usual seats, two or three rows from the back of the church, we were propelled right up to the front where Fr. Dave, in his own inimitable style, welcomed Sheena into the Christian community to a sustained round of applause from the assembled congregation. Afterwards our parents, friends and neighbours joined us for a celebratory party.

For the first few years of Sheens's life, I was involved in various events. I was very interested in the women's movement and attended many meetings in the city. Nell McCaverty was very vocal at the time and inspired many of us young women to think about our roles in life. In the convent I had been told God was so humble, he had become man but I often thought it would have been much more humble for him to have become a black woman! I became secretary of a group called 'The Childminders' Union'. It had been founded by Marie Sheedy, who was trying get recognition for women working at home. We had lots of good ideas and many meetings but, as always, money was a stumbling block. Another group which a few of us set up was called 'Kiddie Care'. This was more successful. It came into existence because of the isolation many of us felt living in big housing estates with very little adult communication. We would meet in the local I.C.A. hall and bring our pre-school children with us. One of the founder members was Mary Crilly who later went on to be the Director of the 'Cork Rape Crisis Centre'. An off-shoot of ' Kiddie Care' was the 'Douglas Mother and Toddler Group', organised by another aware woman, Anne O'Brien. , which is still thriving to-day. Only recently, I met a woman from Dublin at my local leisure centre who told me the Group had been a life saver for her when she first moved to Cork. In addition to teaching piano, I also taught musicianship at night school and took the role of Musical Director of the local I.C.A. Choir, enjoying success with them at various competitions including the Oireachtas in the National Concert Hall in Dublin. We didn't have an awful lot of money in those days but I was happy and fulfilled with Jim, Claire and Sheena and my new friends and neighbours. I was myself in both body and soul.

One summer, we left Sheena with my parents in Rosslare and with my sister's borrowed tent in the boot, set off on something of a whistle-stop tour across north-eastern France and Belgium to Holland. Making our base in a campsite east of Amsterdam, we squeezed in as much sight-seeing as we could over the next few days. We then drove south to Heidelburg, stopping off en route to visit Beethoven's house in Bonn. Then it was another long drive back to Le Havre, where we arrived practically broke in those pre-ATM days. We always looked forward to the summer holidays. There was plenty of time to be together and enjoy the girls growing up. In 1981 we left Sheena with Eileen, a very good neighbour of ours, who, along with her daughter Niamh, frequently helped us out babysitting. We spent two weeks touring Brittany and the following summer Niamh came with us for a holiday in the Lake District. We thought the terrible world of psychiatry was behind us and the future was bright. How wrong we were.

If the cap fits!

8 DÉJÀ VU.

"It is no measure of health to be well adjusted to a profoundly sick society"

Krishnamurti.

In September 1982, we were plunged back into the-terrible world of psychiatry. I'll never forget an occasion when, in the convent, I took some Panadol tablets. They had had an hallucinatory effect on me and I was very frightened. Now, in I 982, I visited my doctor with an ear infection. I now believe the medication he prescribed for me triggered another hallucinatory response. Emotionally, I had been in good health. September was the start of a new music term and there was a certain amount of organising of classes to be done, but nothing unduly stressful. But one night, I went to bed early and a few hours later, woke up as from a bad dream. I became more elated and was prescribed some Valium by my doctor. However, over the next few days, my thoughts began to race and of course, because at this stage I had a psychiatric 'history', it was soon decided I needed to go back to hospital. After my first terrible experience there, this was the last place I wanted to go.

There was a sense of deja vu as I found myself, in the early hours of the morning sitting beside Mary in an ambulance on the way to hospital. At least this time it wasn't to the isolated Sarsfield Court we were heading but rather to the recently opened Cork Regional Hospital which had a psychiatric wing - GF -attached. This was part of the new trend of trying to integrate the psychiatric service into the mainstream hospital service. So we were admitted to the clean, brightly lit modern GF wing where I recall signing some admission papers. At that stage. I still had faith in the system, not liking it but thinking that there was no alternative. But if there were improvements in the hospital environment the treatment being offered was still the same, namely experimentation with different tablets to try to counter a 'chemical imbalance in the brain', So Mary, like all the other patients, was given medication to "bring her down". I don't remember there being too much by way of 'talk therapy' and while there was some occupational therapy in an added-on prefab building that seemed to be something of an afterthought, the 'medical model' was the predominant treatment on offer. And because the professional 'experts' said so and because, as a layman, I trusted them, I went along with them. Drug treatment was the only way. Any possible negative side-effects were played down or brushed aside. The main thing was to find the right drug and to right the 'chemical imbalance' and all would be well.

I didn't know it then but I know it today. There can be a whole range of the most awful side-effects to all medications, ranging from suicidal thoughts, to hallucinations to other serious physical consequences. When these manifest themselves, they are then considered to be part of the psychiatric 'condition' to be treated with even more medication in a misguided and vicious cycle. On a number of occasions, Mary was overcome by a faint-like weakness which caused her to fall to the ground. The reaction of the nurses, whenever this happened, showed how ignorant they were of these side-effects. Angrily, they would tell her to "Get up!" and not to act like that, as if she had some choice in the matter! On top of that, they would make threats to her that she would not be allowed visitors - emotional blackmail of an emotionally disturbed patient and completely at odds with the best traditions of the general nursing profession. It was as if the nurses went along with all the psychiatrists said. Drugs were best, they were for your good and that was the end of it. There was also the question of 'administrative convenience'. When all the patients took their drugs. life was much easier for the people in charge. There were no scenes, no disturbances and everything went smoothly. And if any of the nurses did have any misgivings, they learned to keep their mouths shut, such was the power of the doctors and the prevailing 'medical model" ethos.

When I was in GF, Jim had two young children to look after and still managed to visit me every day. Our friends and neighbours helped him in every way they could and we will never forget them. For all that time, which turned out to be four months, he never missed a day at school. I don't know how he kept going. The GF wing was modern and the food was an improvement on my last stay but there was still very little to do except watch television, which I found very difficult. Occupational therapy was minimal and very frustrating as sometimes, the therapist would not show up. It was drugs and more drugs which made concentration almost impossible and movement, slow. Jim brought me in a paint-by-numbers of two birds but even that was impossible for me! I was very unhappy and can remember very little kindness from the staff. Some of the nurses resembled cross nuns in the boarding school.

Mary remained in GF for six weeks. I would bring the girls in to visit her and we would walk across to the shop in the general wing of the hospital. After a while, she was allowed out for a day or home at weekends. She was meticulous in doing what she was told. If she was to be back for seven o'clock. she wouldn't be a second late even though she always hated going back. And whatever tablets she was given, she took them exactly as prescribed and exactly at the time she was told to take them. At the time, it was in her nature do as she was told, as indeed, it was mine, especially when told by 'experts' in white coats. That willingness to conform unquestioningly to authority was a feature of Irish life in general in the mid-twentieth century and specifically of the Church-dominated educational system of which we were both   products. Today, things are different in every sense. However, even then we began to question the hospital, if not the treatment. We were both becoming more and more frustrated at the ongoing situation.

Mary was in good form most of the time, but subject to the fainting-like episodes which always seemed to set her back, especially given the reaction of the nurses. She was also continually restless, unable to concentrate or read a book, always having to be active. If walking in the autumn sunshine, she would experience excessive burning of her skin. In many respects, she was as she had been that Easter in Donegal before she went to St. Pat's in Dublin. And because she had got better there and had pleasant enough memories of the good occupational therapy facilities, we both decided to give it another try, knowing, even as we decided, that the drug treatment there would be essentially the same as in Cork. There was also the fact that she would be away from the girls and myself but it was a measure of her frustration and desire to be well, that she was prepared to sacrifice our daily visits and those of her other friends in Cork. So, on the Tuesday of the Halloween mid- term break, having made the necessary transfer arrangements, I packed Claire and Sheena into the car, picked up Mary and set off for Dublin.

Even though I had been there before, the locked, antiquated Admission Ward in St. Pat's hit me like a bomb. I was kept there much longer than in 1976. For a person in the whole of their health, it was a depressing place, not to speak about someone emotionally unwell! Some patients sat or lay on their beds, others wandered around. some in docile fashion, others more animated. One young anorexic girl sat up in bed with a plate of food constantly in front of her, which the nurses encouraged her to eat. She was threatened that if she refused her food. her family would not be allowed to visit her as if she hadn't enough to cope with! I was often kept awake at night as the nurses chatted away to themselves. They spent little time talking to the patients. They didn't seem to see this as their role at all. I received no counselling whatsoever in St. Pat's. I was a case of "chemical imbalance" in the brain. I was told it was genetic and could only be treated chemically. 1 believed the 'experts' and did everything 1 was told including submitting myself to yet more ECT. sessions.

John and Catherine, Jim's brother and sister-in-law came to visit me often and brought along Sheena, as they were minding her at this time. She would join me in the bed and never want to leave. It was always terrible when she had to go. My mother also visited me as often as she could. One day she came armed with her crochet hook because she knew I was so restless and needed something to do. She had little to eat as she stayed with me for most of the day. My friends Maura, Una and Sally came on the long journey from Cork and they all had young children to look after too. After a few weeks, I progressed to the downstairs ward and not too long afterwards, was allowed out for weekends though I was cautioned not to rush things as it could result in an even longer stay, the very last thing I wanted.

Not long after she was admitted, Mary's psychiatrist informed me she had diagnosed Mary as having 'hypo-mania' and she suggested a course of E.C.T. Once again, I felt this was the 'expert's' advice and trusted her, never imagining a doctor would dream of doing anything harmful. Following Mary's period in hospital in 1976, we had both gone to see the film One Flew Over the Cuckoo's Nest. I must say 1 was reluctant to see it, thinking it would only re-awaken unpleasant memories for Mary. However, she was very eager to view it and so we went along. It was an excellent film depicting life in a mental hospital in the US in the 1960's. It included a very disturbing scene in which E.C.T. was administered to the main character McMurphy, superbly played by Jack Nicholson. No anaesthetic was used in the procedure and McMurphy was shown, strapped to a couch, having an electric current being applied to his head, causing his body to jerk with violent muscular spasms. It was awful.

While Mary had been given E.C.T. in Sarsfield Court in 1976, I had never witnessed the procedure or had never fully appreciated its impact. I had been assured the treatment was safe, that she would be anaesthetised and would feel nothing, that there would only be some drowsiness and headache afterwards but that it would all be worthwhile, given the benefits that would follow. Now in St. Pat's, six years later, I was given the same advice. Mary had now been in hospital nearly ten weeks since her first admission to the Regional in Cork. How long more was this to go on? If the 'expert' doctor thought E.C.T was necessary, then, desperately and reluctantly, I accepted the recommendation. So, over the next fortnight, Mary was given more sessions of what I would now call, this barbaric treatment. Crudely put, it is like giving a broken television a bang in the hope of restoring the picture. Sometimes it might work but exactly how, is not known. But how anybody could ever think of administering an electric current sufficient to provoke a grand mal convulsion, of inducing a seizure, could be a 'good' treatment for any condition, amazes me. Like earlier 'recommended' barbaric psychiatric treatments such as insulin-induced coma and lobotomy, E.C.T, which has been described as electrical lobotomy, should be banned. Instead, incredibly, it is still practised in Irish hospitals today!

Just before Christmas, Mary was deemed well enough to be discharged. Though still heavily medicated, we were all delighted she was coming home. After the long journeys up and down from Cork with Claire every weekend, we all set off on what we hoped would be our last trip back to

Cork. Claire and Sheena were delighted to have their Mom back with them and their joy was complete because Mary had won a lovely hand-crafted and decorated Wendy House, made by a patient in the hospital and the first prize in the Christmas Raffle. Was Lady Luck beginning to smile on us at last?

With Claire and Sheena, Christmas 1983

9 MANIC-DEPRESSIVE.

"Giving oneself addictive drugs is a crime. Accepting addictive drugs from a 'maintenance programme'is a treatment.

Thomas Szasz.

Returning to 'real life' after three months in hospital was very demanding. I still felt out of things, especially if I was shopping in the supermarket. I was still on medic- ation but resumed my piano lessons in the new year. We always had two birthdays in January - Sheena who was now 3 on the 4th and Claire who was now 7 on the 27th. Sheena was old enough to come on her first holiday with the family the following June. We drove up to spend a week in a hotel in Donegal where we were joined by Jim's parents. It was a wonderful week of fine weather, good food, sight-seeing, swimming, evening walks listening to the rare sound of the corncrake, cross-border trips to Derry and Strabane, games of snooker and crazy-golf, fun and laughter, memories made all the more precious because just a week later, Jim's father died after a stroke. We were all very close to him and missed him greatly.

Life was still stressful enough with two small children, keeping house and teaching piano. That September I became elated again and was referred to a man described at the time as 'the best psychiatrist in Cork'. Not surprisingly, with my history, I soon found myself being admitted to yet another psychiatric hospital. I will always remember going up the terrazzo steps of St. Anne's for the first time. The coldness of those steps symbolised everything about the system I was only too familiar with at this stage though I did experience exceptional kindness from one particular nurse who helped to make my five week stay a little easier. Like me, she loved music and played the guitar and our sessions together, along with some good occupational therapy and twenty cigarettes a day, helped to keep me 'sane'!

As usual, I put my trust in 'the best psychiatrist in Cork' when he admitted Mary to St. Anne's. He was the 'expert'. There was one stipulation I was adamant about, however. That was that I didn't want Mary to have any more E.C.T. It was a welcome development to hear that he agreed. Initially, Mary was put into the locked Admission Ward on the first floor. My experience of the nursing staff there was that they did their job as trained to do and as directed by the system. They saw to the patients, observed and reported their behaviour, administered the drugs and were generally friendly, provided they got co-operation. Any signs of rebellion however, were met with threats of removal to 'Kevin's 3', a particularly forbidding high security wing of the nearby Victorian fortress that was Our Lady's Hospital for long-stay patients.

After a few weeks in St. Anne's, I had a phone call from the psychiatrist. He had diagnosed Mary as having 'a bi-polar mood disorder' which he called manic- depression. Despite earlier diagnoses of 'puerperal psychosis' and 'hypo-mania', both of which I tended to dismiss as so much medical jargon, the term 'manic- depression' had more of an impact on me, particularly the word 'manic' with all its frightening and weird connotations. Mary was elated yes, but I would never have described her as manic. Bowing to his expertise, I listened as he outlined his proposed treatment of starting Mary on lithium, an elementary metallic salt, he explained, but something I had never heard of. He extolled it as a most effective treatment for stabilising the mood-swings of manic-depression. There were two side effects to be aware of and they were that it could affect the functioning of the thyroid gland and the kidneys. Its administration would have to be closely monitored and this would require regular blood tests which would also ascertain that the drug would be maintained at therapeutic levels of between 0.5 and 1.3 millimoles per litre. I don't recall any stress being laid on other side effects. In fact, as I was to later learn, there are many other negative and harmful consequences to taking lithium.

A common comparison at the time and one which is still made today, was that it was like a diabetic having to take daily doses of insulin, a spurious comparison which is part of psychiatry's promotion of lithium.

Mary's manic-depression, I was told, was 'a biological mood disorder' caused by 'a chemical imbalance in the brain' and not only would lithium correct this imbalance and stabilise her moods, but it would help prevent any more breakdowns in the long-term. So the lithium treatment in the form of 500mgs of Camcolit in the morning and a further 250mgs in the evening, began along with the regular blood tests, a regime that was to continue for the next 18 years. In November, she was discharged with instructions not to just keep taking the lithium but also to keep taking two other powerful chloropromazine drugs, Largactil and Surmontil, which were also deemed essential for her continuing and future 'well-being'.

When I was told I was a 'manic-depressive', I took the title on board and tried to make it less shocking. I thought that because I really was a 'normal' person, people would begin to perceive a 'manic-depressive' like anyone else. It was always supposed to be a consolation that a lot of famous and talented people had the same title! When it was proposed to go on the lithium, I believed all the arguments in its favour. Then, I had never heard of Dr. Peter Breggin, the brave American psychiatrist and Harvard graduate, who, for years has challenged his own profession and the powerful drugs industry. His basic message is that there is no research evidence to support the belief that there are mental illnesses with a biological basis and that the physical treatments of drugs and E.C.T. are harmful. In his book 'Toxic Psychiatry', this is what he says about lithium:

"John Cade accidentally discovered the effect of lithium while injecting it into guinea pigs in his laboratory in Australia. Serendipitously he noticed that the guinea pigs became sedated and even flaccid. As he explained in the 1949 Medical Journal of Australia, A noteworthy result was that after a latent period of about two hours the animals, although fully conscious, became extremely lethargic and non- responsive to stimuli for one to two hours before once again becoming normally active and timid.' Notice that the animals became 'extremely lethargic and unresponsive to stimuli.' Does this sound like the discovery of a treatment specific for a 'biochemical imbalance' in manic patients? It is, in fact, the now familiar brain-disabling effect we first saw described in regard to the lobotomising impact of the neuro- leptics (tranquilizing, anti-psychotic drugs). Because this is so disillusioning, the typical textbook of psychiatry makes no mention of the many studies of lithium effects on animals and the average psychiatrist knows little or nothing about it. After this unexpected finding in guinea pigs, did Cade then set up a series of scientifically controlled studies in animals? No need for that, when he had ready access to human guinea pigs in the local state mental hospital. He quickly discovered that he could subdue hospital inmates as easily as he did the guinea pigs, making them into more docile inmates. He himself admitted in his pioneering report that the drug produced a non-specific levelling effect. 'An important feature was that, although there was no fundamental improvement in any of them, three who were usually restless, noisy and shouting nonsensical abuse … lost their excitement and restlessness and became quiet and amenable for the first time in years.' Yet Cade would later call lithium a 'magic wand' for mania."

I was one of these guinea pigs and remained on lithium for over 15 years afterwards. I was scared to even miss one tablet as I thought this was the only way I could avoid a return visit to a psychiatric hospital and be taken away again from my husband, children and friends. I believed the psychiatrists were the 'experts'.

10 SIDE EFFECTS.

"Of all tyrannies, a tyranny sincerely exercised for the good of its victims may be the most oppressive."

C.S. Lewis.

On leaving St. Anne's, I still continued to visit my psychiatrist for regular, private consultations. His practice was to have his secretary first collect the substantial fee and then for me to wait, along with other patients, up to two hours before he would see me for what never was longer than ten minutes. I would talk about the girls' progress in school and then my medication would be briefly discussed, though rarely altered from the 50mgs of Largactil, 100mgs of Surmontil and the 750mgs of Camcolit. The regularity of the visits reminded me of confession when I was young. "I told lies, I didn't do what I was told, I didn't say my morning and night prayers." If this was the right way to be treated, I don't know why it was necessary to visit him at all as it could all have been done over the phone. But of course, there was the small matter of the fee.

After only a year on this cocktail of drugs, my weight shot up from under 9 stone to over 11 stone. I am only 5 feet high. Eventually, I reached 13 stone. Movement became slow and difficult, going uphill left me out of breath. Bending down or working in our sloping back garden became impossible, a past-time I had greatly enjoyed. My extra weight contributed to a womb prolapse. My kidneys deteriorated year by year until I was visiting the bathroom at least three times during the night. I experienced severe stomach cramps and gripe pains which frequently disturbed my sleep. I developed a constant shake in my hand which meant I could no longer enjoy painting, another hobby of mine. I was physically incapable of getting up any day before mid-day. When I mentioned these effects to my psychiatrist, his only suggestion was to take the medication earlier in the evening, never to take any less. When I questioned why I had to take Largactil (a downer) and Surmontil (an upper) simultaneously, I only received a lot of medical jargon in reply.

I n school, I had studied Honours Maths for my Leaving Cert. and difficult harmony for my Music Diploma. Now I couldn't concentrate, follow a film plot or motivate myself to learn any new music. Only my years of practice enabled me to continue with my piano lessons, though in a very mechanical fashion. I had very little environmental awareness and could easily get lost. My driving steadily got worse and I was involved in an accident, fortunately not too serious. I subsequently drove very little and became more of a prisoner in my home. I didn't feel capable of even going to Dublin by myself on the train. I was like a child. Sometimes, I would wake around 2 o'clock at night with terrible racing thoughts, one of the worst aspects of my so- called 'illness'. I became more and more dependent on Jim and because of these racing thoughts, couldn't bear for him to leave the house, even for a single night. I always wished I would die before him as I thought I could never survive by myself. This was all my 'illness'. I had to bear it. There was no other way other than stopping my medication which my 'expert' doctor wouldn't hear about.

Looking back now, there were indeed certain Orwellian aspects to life as we commenced the year 1984. There was a degree of 'double-speak' on my own part as well as her psychiatrist in describing Mary as 'well'. Because she was able to resume work, because she was able to carry out her functions as a mother and housewife but most of all because she was not in hospital, we said that Mary was well. Yes, she continued to visit the psychiatrist who continued to prescribe the medication but the 'success' of this treatment was always celebrated with claims that her manic-depression was now under control, that her moods had been stabilised and, best of all, that she no longer had to be in hospital. Understandably, we accepted this official line. Certainly we didn't want to re-visit or re-live the night-marish hell of any further three or four month stays in mental hospitals - anything but that and a few tablets in the morning and a few more in the evening seemed an acceptable price to pay. 'Did you take your tablets?' assumed the nature of a mantra over the following years.

Mary acquired a special pill-box in which she organised her daily doses on a weekly basis, a regime she adhered to with religious meticulousness.

When travelling or on holiday, great care had to be taken to have a back-up supply in case the first one was lost. Believing at the time, the comparison of lithium with insulin, to not take it, to forget to take it or to be unable to take it because you had lost it, would have had the most awful consequences. So a dependency was built up, aided and abetted by me, by her psychiatrist and also by our involvement in an organisation which, at the time, we were very glad to be part of.

The organisation was 'Aware', a support group founded by Dr. Patrick McKeown of St. Patrick's Hospital, Dublin. With its optimistic logo of the sun coming out to shine from behind a cloud and its sub-title 'Helping to defeat Depression', 'Aware' was and continues even still to be a high profile flagship in the mental health area. It runs an annual fund-raising week advertised by well-known people like RTE celebrities Anne Doyle and Marion Finucane. It publishes a quarterly magazine and promotes the formation of further branches throughout the provinces. It undoubtedly does good work in bringing mental health issues out into the open and in helping to educate the general public in an effort to reduce the concomitant stigma. In Cork, we became regular attenders at the monthly meetings of the local branch. There were two separate support groups, one for former patients, the other for family members and both were helpful in trying to come to terms with our situation. But central to the philosophy of 'Aware' was the absolute need for people to continue with their medication. Warnings were given that, despite feeling they could do without drugs, there would be a greatly increased risk of a further breakdown for anyone who 'stopped taking the tablets'.

I don't recall much if any discussion on the issue of side effects. Even the term itself reflected the official thinking. Side effects were just that - side effects- 'mild' or 'temporary' - a minor factor not worthy of any great consideration given the generally accepted major benefits to be had from the medication. For Mary, as I said, these included being back at work and being out of hospital. She was able to cope with the ordinary things of life again. Sheena started school, Claire made her First Communion. In the summer, we went on holidays again. In 1986, we carried out a major house extension. That same year, we also undertook the first of a series of home-exchange holidays with a family from the south of France. Always very house proud, these exchanges imposed an added degree of pressure in organising and preparing for our guests. Because she coped with all these situations, I too considered her 'well'. But subtly and stealthily, Mary was changing before my very eyes, even though I didn't see it. Today, when I look at a photo of her in 1976 and another in 1993, I wonder how I could have been so blind. Maybe it was because it was slow and gradual, a case of not seeing the wood for the trees. And it wasn't that I was totally blind. I could see for example, that she never got out of bed any day until after mid-day. I would get the girls up and out to school in the morning but I thought it no big deal if she wanted to stay on in bed. Before she ever met me, she had always described herself as a 'night person' able to stay up late but different in the morning. But the reality now was that she was physically incapable of getting up before mid-day, so zonked out was she from her medication taken the evening before. But as I said, I didn't consider it a big deal. An inevitable consequence however, was that she began to put on weight.

Again, because it was gradual, I didn't think too much of it, something that happened to all of us as we got older. But the reality again was that these changes were all part of the rarely-mentioned side effects of her drug cocktail. She began to develop a tremor in her hand, so bad it was impossible to hold a glass or a cup. Her hair began to thin to such an extent you could see her scalp. Her skin tingled with a terrible itch in the sunshine. She suffered severe cramps. But worst of all she began to experience hallucinatory episodes from time to time at night. We could never say when they might occur other than when they did, it was always around the same time - 2 o'clock in the early hours. Even though fast asleep, I would instinctively know when one of these episode would occur. I would wake up to find Mary sitting on the side of the bed in a shocked, dazed and frightened state. She could never clearly relate the specific detail of the dream/nightmare/hallucination she had endured other than saying it included, in the crazy, illogical way such things do, frightening and awful flashes relating to family, friends and acquaintances in her life. The experience was terrifying. I would sense it the instant I awoke. My own heart would pump madly. Was this the beginning of another breakdown? Mary would sit in a semi-trance like fashion, obviously shaken and shocked.. A few minutes later, she would begin to be herself again, saying she was alright but still deeply un-nerved by the experience. Fortunately, Claire and Sheena always continued sleeping in their rooms next door. Mary would eventually fall asleep again but when she awoke after mid-day the following day, would always feel drained and completely exhausted.

Whenever we mentioned these episodes to her psychiatrist, he was very dismissive and completely played them down. There was never any mention of them being a possible side effect of the medication or of changing the medication in any way. From his point of view, she was able to get over these 'little episodes', she was able to continue working and the main thing, she was able to stay out of hospital. He would write out a repeat prescription for three further months supply of the drugs, enquire briefly about the girls and arrange another appointment for three months later. For the next 15 years, she continued to visit this man every three to six months and continued to have her regular lithium blood tests. She also continued to put on weight. In addition, she now began to walk with her arms held stiffly at her side. She began to have a whitish discharge from the side of her mouth, particularly in bed. She began to find it increasingly difficult to drive the car. Her mind became fogged so that she found it difficult to observe landmarks or follow directions. She was apprehensive about using an ATM machine. She found it hard to follow the plot of a film. She had now entered a kind of twilight world with her sensations and emotions greatly numbed.

In 1989 her father died. A naturally stressful time, I was concerned about how his death would hit her but she glided through the experience in robotic fashion. In 1990 we arranged a house-swap in New Hampshire, U.S.A. It was the first time any of us had been to America. Claire, Sheena and I were all wildly excited but not Mary. And the night-time hallucinations were still continuing. They struck without warning on a random basis, the only constant being the same time - 2 o'clock in the early hours. They struck at home and away. I can recall an episode in London in 1988 and again that summer in New Hampshire in 1990. They could happen a week later or sometimes, not for months later. But they were always there. They never went away and even though it was staring us in the face, we never realised the reason for them until after events which happened in the summer of 1993.

Thirteen stone

11 TURNING POINT.

"Life breaks us all sometimes and some people grow stronger from the broken pieces."

Unknown.

At the beginning of June, we had s short holiday break in Brittany. It was only on the ferry to Cherbourg that I realised I had forgotten our passports. I really should have kept my mouth shut, but long term, as things worked out, was very glad I didn't. When I told Mary, she became very anxious and worried lest there would be problems with immigration officials when we arrived In France. In the event, we were not even asked for them as we drove out of the port and south to Dinan where we had booked a hotel for a few nights. That night Mary woke up with one of her awful hallucinatory episodes. As per usual, the next day she felt utterly drained and a few nights later, she experienced another. When we arrived back in Rosslare at the end of the week, she went to bed in my mother's house only to wake up at 2am with yet another episode. The next day she was physically exhausted and at the same time very anxious. On arriving back in Cork, we immediately went to see her psychiatrist, such as our faith was still in the man at that time. Quite elated at this stage, she was admitted to St. Anne's for a few days. Her dosage of Largactil was increased but her Surmontil was immediately stopped. On discharge, she was told to continue with her Lithium and Largactil which of course, being the compliant patient she always was, she did. She continued to suffer the same terrible side effects but with one very notable exception.

Remarkably, the awful night-time hallucinations stopped! Always apprehensive lest they re-appeared out of the blue, she experienced none for a few months, then for a year, then for a few years and eventually none ever again in the twelve years since. And they had stopped when she had stopped taking the Surmontil. Could anything have been more obvious? It was a major turning point on her road to recovery, the happy end product of forgetting our passports on that fateful day in June, 1993. To have that terrible fear, which could and had struck at random over the previous ten years, removed and to be able to go to bed, secure in the knowledge it was gone, was a huge, huge relief to both of us. The scales eventually were beginning to fall from our eyes.

Not that everything was fine now. In the psychiatric world, Mary was still a 'manic- depressive' and she still had to maintain her regime of Largactil and Lithium with their concomitant side effects. Her weight continued to increase, she still experienced severe stomach cramps and nausea, she couldn't stand exposure to the sun, she still had a shake in her hands, her libido decreased and her brain still seemed to be in a fogged state. She continued to visit her psychiatrist every six months until he died but continued, under his successor, with her usual medication.

It was while attending Aware meetings that I first met Helena, a fellow so called 'manic- depressive'. A spirited and intelligent woman, she was well read and well informed on the world of psychiatry, a fact that did not always go down well at the Aware meetings, especially when she raised the issue of medication and side effects. In fact, I can remember urging her to 'keep taking her medication' to stabilise her moods, just as I was doing! I didn't fully appreciate her at the time, but today I can say that meeting Helena was another significant milestone on my journey to recovery. Throughout the nineties we became good friends and it was she who introduced me to the writing of the remarkable Dr. Peter Breggin and his book 'Toxic Psychiatry'. While it made some sense to me then, I didn't understand or appreciate it fully because of the effects of the drugs I was still taking. Nevertheless, here was a man who was questioning the whole business of taking medication and indeed many of the basic beliefs of the psychiatric establishment itself. Combined with my own experience of that world, and especially my encounters with Surmontil, a seed was being sown. But being still caught in that world, being still branded a 'manic- depressive', it was still going to be difficult to gain my liberation. I too still 'kept taking the tablets.'

Paradoxically, this proved to be a third step on my journey to recovery.

The results of taking medication for nearly 20 years had resulted in me becoming a bloated, overweight woman of 13 stone. I am only 5 feet in height and my original weight had been under 9 stone. At 50 years of age, I now developed a prolapsed womb to add to my other troubles. Fortunately, I did not have to have a hysterectomy as my gynaecologist was able to rectify the matter by inserting a ring but this would only be effective if I lost weight, which he strongly urged me to do. With this motivation, I now began to take some regular exercise. Every day for about 15 minutes, I walked up and down the hills of the estate where we lived. After six months I had lost about half a stone and felt fit enough to graduate to an hour every morning as I did the four mile return trip to Douglas. I was now meeting some of my walking neighbours and began to make new friends in the area. Two of them, Mary and Rose, became regular companions as we clocked up the miles in all kinds of weather, discussing all kinds of topics at the same time. They were both very interested in my story and gave me a lot of good, sound advice. Mary was a nurse who had lived in America for 10 years while Rose had lived in Germany for almost 30 years and was a firm believer in natural remedies. Two other dear friends, a second nurse called Mary and the bubbly Aileen were also a great positive influence on my life, encouraged me all the way and helped me to discover myself again. When I met them I was still 12 stone and taking the drugs. Jim, Claire and Sheena were also a great support. Ironically, Claire was now in England studying pharmacy while Sheena had opted to study alternative medicine. Feeling physically and mentally much better, talking to more people, informing myself more and more, I now began to think in terms of gradually reducing my daily dose of Largactil.

Under the supervision of my doctor, I initially cut out 10mgms every second day for a prolonged period. I then cut it out altogether before repeating the procedure slowly and carefully over the next four years. The benefits gradually became noticeable. I lost the shake in my hand, I could walk in the sun-shine without the awful tingling sensation, my stomach cramps began to wane, the whitish discharge from my mouth stopped, I could get up earlier in the morning and most of all, I felt the re-awaking of my spirit and zest for life. Music really began to mean something to me again. Jim would join me walking at weekends and we began to discover the lovely trails around the shore of Lough Mahon, along the Marina, along the old Blackrock railway line, along the banks of the Ownabue in Carrigaline, Skiddy's walk in Kinsale and many, many more. Another was along the new, as yet unopened road down to the Jack Lynch Tunnel under the Lee, then under construction and there was the memorable opening day in 1999, when, along with thousands of other citizens of the city, we first walked through the Tunnel, with all the proceeds going to local charities. Looking back now, that tunnel walk takes on a new significance. At last we were beginning to emerge from the darkness of the previous 16 years.

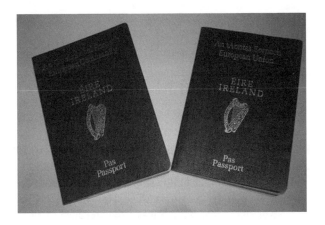

A fortuitous event!

12 OVERCOMING FEAR.

" The only thing we have to fear is fear itself"

F. D. Roosevelt.

When I was diagnosed as a so-called 'manic-depressive' in 1983, I was given a booklet entitled 'Lithium: A Practical Guide' published by The Mood Disorder Fellowship of Ireland. It has a question and answer format. One of the questions asked 'How long will I be taking lithium?' The answer stated that lithium was a maintenance medication and was usually taken indefinitely, much as a person with diabetes would take insulin. It also stated that anyone stopping their lithium would have a 70% chance of a major depression or manic episode within the first six months of stopping treatment. Jim and I had accepted this message from the 'expert professionals', underscored as it was with its threat of fear, for almost 20 years.

But in 'Toxic Psychiatry', Peter Breggin was expressing another view of lithium. Challenging the psychiatric establishment's claim that it was a 'magic bullet', he wrote "After experiments were done on some 'normal volunteers' who received lithium, studies showed a general dulling and blunting of various personality functions and overall slowing of cognitive processes. The normal volunteers were observed by trained mental health professionals as well as by a 'significant other' such as a girl-friend or room-mate. The significant others recognised lithium's dulling and alienating impact on their companions, including 'increased levels of drowsiness and lowered ability to work hard and to think clearly'. The trained mental health professionals - what did they observe? They were 'unable to detect any behavioural changes in the subjects induced by lithium. Mental health professionals are trained - but trained to what end? They conveniently are taught not to notice the dangerous impact of their treatments. This is true whether we are talking about lobotomy, electroshock or drugs. Normal volunteers or patients taking lithium won't necessarily realise how impaired they have become. One reason why lithium serum levels must be taken periodically is that the drugged patients lose their judgement about their impaired state. Frequently they don't notice or report symptoms such as the obvious tremor or skin rash. This inattention to harmful drug effects reflects the psychological indifference or apathy produced by the medication, a reaction that worsens with larger and more dangerous doses. Hardly the anticipated 'magic bullet'!

For all the years I was taking lithium - 750mgms every day - I had to attend for regular blood tests at the Outpatient Clinic in St. Anne's. On one occasion however, I had a test done while attending my GP for some other matter, only to be told, to my surprise, that the serum level was below normal. I went back to my psychiatrist and he sent me for another test to St. Anne's. On receiving the result, he told me the reading was fine even though I hadn't increased the dosage. Years later after he had died, I managed, though with great difficulty, to get my records where it said my level was 0.38. The therapeutic level is meant to be between 0.5 and 1.3. I later had my levels monitored by another GP where I discovered that they were always under 0.5. I was unable to get my records from St. Annes's but the experience raised doubts in my mind about the credibility of my psychiatrist, a man whom I had regarded as a life-saver when he, as 'one of the leading psychiatrists in Cork' had taken me on as a patient way back in 1983.

Our credibility in the psychiatric establishment was further stretched when we became involved with The Cork Advocacy Network (CAN). We were not present at the first meeting of CAN, held in Cork in January, 2001 as we simply had not heard about the event. Mary Leland later reported on the meeting in the Sunday Independent. "It is this enigmatic cartel known as the psychiatric services in Ireland which the Cork Advocacy Network was set up to challenge, in the belief, according to spokeswoman Joan Hamilton, that other approaches to the treatment of mental or emotional breakdown are possible and might even be successful. It is the inability or lack of inclination to change among the practitioners - at least as experienced by so many people in the Munster region - which brought more than 600 people to the first meeting of CAN in January 2001. Many voices were raised at that meeting; many terrible stories were told as family members spoke of the impact of depression, schizophrenia or bi-polar disorder on their households.

The CAN campaign is fuelled by the awareness ... that drugs alone, despite their temporary usefulness, cannot be the best treatment, ... that chemicals are not necessarily all, or even part, of the solution. As Joan Hamilton relates their experiences, these parents shared the feeling that the drug treatment they were offered, whilst appearing to help at the time, did nothing to address the cause of the problem. When the patient was discharged without any back-up support or psychosocial help, then the only way to go was back into hospital again. Three out of four admissions to acute psychiatric wards are re-admissions. The Cork Advocacy Network now includes service users among its membership, as well as some concerned service providers who believe that the system has to be changed "from the top."

As a long-term 'service user', this was a movement I was very interested in. Jim and I both began to go along to the CAN meetings and the friends, stories, support and most of all, information we encountered was another important step on my journey to recovery. It was during this time, the spring of 2001, that I first heard of Dr. Terry Lynch. He was being interviewed by Pat Kenny on his radio show about his new book 'Beyond Prozac'. Terry was saying things that made a lot of sense to me. I was very impressed. Shortly afterwards, I read in The Sunday Tribune the headline that made a big difference to my life - 'The Doctor Who Won't Do Drugs' by Annmarie Hourihane. "Terry Lynch thinks that human misery has been over-sold or perhaps sold from the wrong stall. He thinks that natural unhappiness has been re-christened depression, fed with pills no one understands and policed by a medical profession in general and a psychiatric profession in particular, that lives on wishful thinking - Terry Lynch is a doctor."

She went on to say "Lynch's new book is called 'Beyond Prozac - Healing Mental Suffering without Drugs'. At the same time, he begs people not to come off their psychiatric drugs suddenly. 'This should only be done with medical guidance and supervision.' So doctors are part of the problem and part of the solution. It has suited doctors (and indeed all of us) to ascribe mental problems to the realm of mental illness, as if they were abnormal. In fact 25% of the adult population will experience depression in their lifetime. It's our approach that is wrong, according to Lynch. No one knows what really causes depression. It has never been proven that a chemical imbalance in the brain is responsible for depression although that is the most commonly used explanation today."

Yet I was one who had believed this at a terrible cost for most of my adult life!

Terry was further quoted. "I am seriously questioning whether the drugs used against depression work by re-balancing a supposed imbalance. They do work for some people but the amphetamines worked for some people in the 60's and tranquillisers worked for some people in the 70's and 80's. In 1967, 12 million Americans were on amphetamines which had been prescribed by their doctors. There were 23.3 million prescriptions for amphetamines written in America that year. I fear that only the drugs have changed." The article continued "Terry loved being an ordinary GP. The only thing that bothered him was that there were so many problems coming in the door that didn't fit into the medical model. 'I realised that for a huge proportion of my patients, I wasn't trained properly.' He started giving troubled patients more time, did some counselling courses and also trained for a year with psychologist Tony Humphreys who wrote the introduction to his book. What Lynch learned with him 'made more sense than the medical model I had been taught.'

Terry eventually gave up being a GP where he could have been a much wealthier man. He completed a Masters degree in Humanistic and Integrative Psychotherapy and is now working fulltime as a psychotherapist in Limerick - a much better choice in my opinion. If only there were more like him today! I was so inspired and encouraged by the article and the book which of course I had snapped up, that I wanted to thank him personally. I managed to locate his phone number and spoke to him for the first time. I subsequently met him a number of times and the enthusiasm and sincerity of the man was like a good tonic. From the word go, he believed in me as a survivor just as much as I believed in him as a professional and above all as a good thinker, someone who didn't take things at face value and had the courage of his convictions. He listened to me, encouraged me and his great understanding of the psychiatric system greatly helped me. Equally important, he helped and emboldened Jim along the road he too had started to travel and together we will be forever grateful to him.

As I said, when my friend Helena had first given me a copy of Peter Breggin's 'Toxic Psychiatry' I hadn't fully appreciated it. Now free from the stultifying effects of Largactil and inspired by my meetings with Terry, I read it a second time and it was a further revelation to me. Time and time again I had been told over the preceding 20 years that I had a 'chemical imbalance' in my brain, that I was 'manic-depressive' and that drugs were the answer. But like Terry Lynch, Peter Breggin too was saying that there was no convincing evidence to support such claims of the medical-pharmaceutical establishment. More than that, he was also saying that patients were not being told that the 'miracle' cures they were being prescribed were much less effective and in fact, were more dangerous than they realized! The more I read, the more I was becoming converted. It was frightening and at the same time illuminating to read what he had to say about the whole range of psychiatric drugs, including the ones I had experience of - Surmontil, Largactil and lithium. Now the fear factor used by the professionals to get you to take the tablets was being countered by another -- the fear of serious damaging effects, both mental and physical, that followed from long-term use of them. I knew what he was saying \was right but, at the back of my mind, I was still scared 'they' might be right. I was still scared of the psychiatric hospital. Initially, Jim wasn't as convinced as I was but along with Terry, Peter Breggin had opened his eyes to the reality of the 'medical model'. I got him to promise that no matter what, I would never return to a psychiatric hospital. I had to be sure. Most people believed that I should continue with the lithium but I was now beginning to think if I didn't need Surmontil and Largactil, that I was feeling much better without them and their side effects, that maybe I could do without lithium too. But the power of the 'medical model' still had some hold on me.

Then something happened that helped me to finally make up my mind. Jim had a friend who had also been taking lithium for many years. He now became toxic and was admitted to intensive care where he almost died. I went to visit him in hospital. He had to come off lithium cold turkey as it was affecting some of his vital organs. A psychiatrist called Dr. Browne was attending him at the time and I heard that he wasn't completely closed to the idea of people coming off. On a balmy summer's evening, Jim and I went to see him. He was about to retire and I would have been one of the last people he saw. In the course of a two hour visit in which we, and especially he, talked about many things, he gave me his blessing and told me to wean myself off. Even then, despite everything, I had to have the approval of a psychiatrist. I thank him as he was open enough to help me on that summer's evening.

The difficult job then was to do it, even though I took it more slowly than Dr. Browne had suggested. I was lucky that another friend of mine, Padrigin, a doctor, was coming to me for music lessons every week. She offered me great support and encouragement. From my daily dose of

750mgs, I initially cut out one tablet of 250mgs. At the beginning especially, I would feel very weak from time to time and sometimes at night I would wake up with a terrible physical weakness so bad I thought I was going to die! This was not anything like the hallucinations I experienced when taking the Surmontil but it raised fears in me and reawakened memories of those awful times. This was a more physical thing. I felt like my body was being drained of all my strength and somehow drifting away from me.

My sleep pattern was consequently very disturbed. Occasionally, I would experience the same feelings in the daytime. I endured constant bouts of nausea. Unfortunately, it was a time which coincided with me going through the menopause and its attendant severe hot flushes. All in all, it was quite a physical ordeal but what kept me going was the knowledge that I was a walking physical time-bomb were I to continue on the lithium. For three months I continued to dispense with one daily 250mgs tablet. Slowly, the physical effects I was suffering began to lessen. For the next three months, I dispensed with a second tablet. In hindsight, I think it would have been better to have taken the whole weaning off process even more slowly. Padrigin was a great support for me. She had known me from school days and had known the lively and spirited girl I once was. Altogether, over the total period of 18 years I had been taking lithium, I calculate that I must have swallowed over 5 kilograms! I'm sorry now I can't remember the exact date, but there came a day in the spring of 2001 when I took my last tablet of lithium. While I am writing this, Peer Gynt's 'Morning' is on in the background and it suggests beautifully my liberation. Now I was truly free to be myself again after almost 20 years of chemical lobotomy. You can only imagine the feeling!

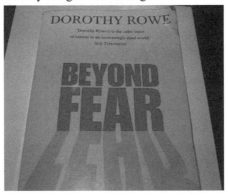

13 WATER, WATER.

" The secret of health for both mind and body is not to mourn for the past, worry about the future or anticipate troubles but to live in the present moment visibly and earnestly."

Buddah.

As I said, Peer Gynt's 'Morning' now had an extra significance for me. For all those years on my cocktail of drugs, mornings had passed me by. Never being able to physically arise until after mid-day, I was missing out on so much of what life has to offer. Now, being completely drug-free, I could really experience the phrase President Jimmy Carter had once used in relation to the middle-east conflict- namely, the 'miracle of an ordinary life.'

I had already started walking on a regular basis, doing over twenty miles a week. I began to loose a lot of weight - two stone in the first two years. Everyone was seeing me in a new light and commenting on this all the time. In the summer of 2001, Jim and I had a holiday in Germany. We hired a car for two weeks and explored what had formerly been East Germany. We visited Berlin, Dresden and the enchanting, medieval town of Quedlinburg, a world heritage town previously unknown to us. We concluded with a relaxing stay in a small hotel in Bad Toltz, a picturesque Bavarian spa town in the foothills of the Alps, just south of Munich. It was here in the pool of the Beer Kursanitorium, which translates as "Beer wellness hotel" (Beer being the family name!) that I re-discovered the therapeutic effects of swimming, something I hadn't done for years. I had been so conscious of my thirteen stone, I couldn't contemplate being seen in a swimsuit. I had never been a good swimmer and had always kept my head out of the water. Even in the shower, I couldn't bear water on my face! But during that week in Bavaria, I began to discover the relaxing qualities of water and decided to further explore them when I returned home.

There was a Health and Leisure Club attached to The Maryborough Hotel which was only a few minutes drive away. Jim and I enrolled as 'off-peak pool members' which suited our purposes. Soon after joining, I met Valerie from Cobh who was one of the pool instructors. At the time, she was starting up an 'aqua-robics' class so I thought I might join, not knowing much about it except it was exercise in the water to music. I had always loved dancing so I thought this would be the next best thing. What can I say about Valerie? She is one of those exceptional people you only meet very rarely. Her enthusiasm, energy and sense of fun was infectious. On three mornings a week we had our classes. They were tough but very enjoyable. I got to know the other women and a genuine club atmosphere was developed. Valerie organised nights out at Christmas and a few 'away' trips to West Cork which were great fun. I developed the routine of going to the pool every morning. Valerie gave me lots of tips and assistance, especially with my arm and leg movements, including 'Charlie Chaplin's stand! Denise, a daughter of a neighbour and one of my music pupils, taught me how to breath under water and I was no longer afraid of the water on my face. Now, having no trouble getting up in the morning, I sometimes had the whole pool to myself with some lovely, relaxing background music. Often I would bring some of my own favourite 'c.d's which Valerie would play for me. It was bliss. People often told me I was great to be so disciplined to get up early and go off to the pool every morning but to me, after all my mornings zonked out 'til after mid-day, it was just such a joy and pleasure. And because I was making such constant use of the pool, it was costing me just a euro a day!

At this time too, I also enrolled in a practical philosophy course with my friend Maura. Here, we learned about living in the moment and concentrating on the senses as a form of relaxation. From a situation of fearing water on my face, I now positively loved the gentle, therapeutic lapping of the water as I floated in a literal and metaphorical state of complete relaxation or listened, with heightened awareness, to the soothing sounds of the jacuzzi. Learning to swim properly and doing all the exercises in the aqua-robics demanded very good concentration and this in turn helped me to relax more and more. When I was on drugs, I had always been so tense that my teeth were often clenched.

Of course, my new way of life greatly helped my self-esteem, boosted my confidence and gave me new faith in myself. You actually begin to like yourself. This to me is the basis for good, sound mental and physical health. I was being empowered, thanks to Valerie and the kind staff in the club, who helped me to help myself. The psychiatric world, as I had experienced it, had done the opposite. It always wanted to control and make others powerless. Based on fear and a regime of drug maintenance, it offers little by way of 'recovery'. But it is when we pass 'beyond fear' as the renowned psychologist Dorothy Rowe says in her book of the same name, that we are truly empowered and liberated. We can get to know ourselves, we can go beyond our fear and face life with courage.

Bliss!

14 ANGER.

" Injustice anywhere is a threat to justice everywhere"

M. Luther King

Liberated and all as I now was, this still wasn't going to be a story with a happy-ever-after ending. Yes, it was great to be at last drug-free, to have a clear mind and to feel I was living life again. But all of this was accompanied by another powerful emotion - anger.

I suppose it was a kind of post-traumatic stress - a natural response made all the more forceful the more I realised what I had endured over the preceding twenty years - the awfulness of the hospitals, the early separation from Claire, the forced injections, the ECT, the locked doors, the long months of separation from Jim, Claire and Sheena when I was in St. Patrick's in Dublin, the haughty and dismissive attitudes of doctors and nurses, the branding with the stigma of labels - puerperal psychosis, hypomania, manic-depression - the terrible side effects of my medication, the restlessness, the fogged mental confusion and the terrible, terrible hallucinations. How had all this happened to me? I was a young woman of 26. I had just married the man I loved. I was having my first baby. It should have been the happiest time of my life. Instead it had turned into a nightmare.

I was angry with Jim. How could he have gone along with it all? He had seen for himself the awful conditions in the hospitals. How could he have given his approval for me to have ECT? How would he have liked to have been branded with the label of 'manic-depressive'? Could he not see what was being inflicted on me? I was befuddled in a fog of chlorpromazine but he wasn't. Why did he not speak out against what was being done to me? Instead, he went along with it all. We had many fights and arguments about it. Jim's defence was always that he was a layman who bowed to the superior knowledge of the 'experts' who were in charge. But I wasn't happy with that. Why was he so compliant? Why did he not shout 'Stop'? He is an avid reader of the newspapers and never misses the news on either radio or television. He would get very animated and annoyed over the issue of sexual abuse by the clergy which dominated the media at this time. I would tell him the issue of psychiatric abuse was every bit as bad if not worse but still he couldn't see that. Doctors were the caring profession, he said. Their job was to help people. They couldn't be equated with paedophiles who deliberately and systematically groomed and abused innocent children. But unintended or not, the net result of the way they treated me was abuse.

Jim was a product of the educational system and societal mores of the Ireland of the 1950's and 1960's. You did what you were told and didn't question people in authority. The church was omnipotent. Politicians and government leaders were still subject to 'the belt of a crozier'. In the rigid hierarchial structure of that society, the medical profession also carried enormous clout. Ironically, Dr. Noel Browne had found that to his cost with his failed Mother and Child Scheme in the early 1950's. While the church has lost much of its authority because of the abuse scandals, there are still many consultants in existence today who regard themselves as 'gods' in their respective spheres. But issues like the Hepatitis C scandal and the Dr. Neary scandal in Drogheda highlight the wrongs that can follow when the 'experts' turn out to have feet of clay. Slowly, Jim's eyes were being opened.

There is no doubt that when it came to my education in the psychiatric system, I was a slow learner. From the beginning, I had accepted what the 'experts' had said. I accepted all the labels Mary was given, I accepted the drug treatment she was given and I always thought that it was all to make her 'better'. That's what doctors did. When I spoke with them, I followed to a tee everything they told me to do - the exact medication to be given, the exact timetable for temporary release, the exact Lithium treatment programme for 'manic-depression' complete with regular visits to consultants and regular blood tests. The only treatment I ever questioned was the ECT and that was only in 1983 after Mary had endured many earlier sessions of the barbaric treatment. My basic instinct told me it was wrong. Any literature I read at the time or any extra information I picked up from my association with Aware, was all grounded in what today is called 'the medical model' of bio-psychiatry. It has no qualms with accepting the term 'mental illness' which it claims is a result of a 'chemical imbalance' in the brain. I had never heard of people like Dr. Peter Breggin nor was I aware of the world of anti-psychiatry that existed out there. I vaguely remember seeing an interview with R.D. Laing on The Late, Late Show but my recollection is of a rambling and incoherent man whose views were given little quarter. To my shame, I never obliged myself to buy any of his books and inform myself what precisely his views were, even if he hadn't made himself clear in the interview with Gay Byrne.

And yes, while I could see the glaring injustices of the church sex-scandals and cover-ups, I was still reluctant to put them in the same category as psychiatry. Yes, I knew that there was much that was wrong in it. I knew the played-down and rarely-mentioned terrible side effects of many of the drugs but the difference I thought was that, unlike the sex abuse, these wrongs in the psychiatric system were not intended. They were part of a medical profession who took a Hippocratic Oath which stated 'First, do no harm'. But of course, priests too swore oaths of chastity at their ordinations.

At this stage, Mary had read and re-read Peter Breggin's 'Toxic Psychiatry' and Terry Lynch's 'Beyond Prozac'. I began to read them too. Both books advanced me rapidly along the path of enlightenment. I had my own empirical knowledge of Mary's experiences with psychiatrists and the side effects of medication, but I had not realised the frightening wider picture which now emerged. I was particularly struck by a quotation from C.S. Lewis, used by Peter Breggin in his first chapter Psychiatry Out of Control. It said "Of all tyrannies, a tyranny sincerely exercised for the good of its victims may be the most oppressive". This was what Mary was trying to get me to see, that irrespective of the intentions, good or otherwise of those in control, the net result was a 'tyranny' every bit as bad, in its worst excesses, as clerical sex abuse or, for that matter, the treatment of the Jews in Nazi Germany.

Ironically, that summer of 2002 as we re-traced the steps of our honeymoon in Bilbao in 1974, could so easily have caused our marriage to break up. We had constant fights over small things like tipping in restaurants which nearly always escalated into major rows to do with the same topic - what had happened to Mary and the way I had reacted. Looking back now, it was, as Mary has said, a 'post-traumatic stress' situation and fortunately, a situation we both managed, though not without a lot of pain and hurt, to survive.

There were pleasant sides to our holiday too. We discovered a small, intimate Basque bar and its few welcoming and friendly regulars in the back streets of Murcia. We searched for but failed to locate the apartment block in Neguri where Mary had worked as an au pair in 1973 and where we had stayed on our honeymoon in 1974. We shopped again in El Gorte Ingles and re-traced our steps along the Calle Santa Maria and around the Cathedral de Santiago in the old town. We later motored on to Laredo on the Cantabrian coast and then turned south to Vittoria in the heart of the Rioja country. When we drove back through San Sebastian and crossed the border at Irun, we especially sought out the old cream-coloured run down hotel with the red shutters where the old wrinkled and stooped woman had shown us to our room with the equally ancient wooden bed 28 years earlier. This time an old Basque man with a black beret and luxuriant moustache told us over a half-door that the hotel had closed many years before but the building itself was still there as indeed were the red shutters.

This time we didn't have to stand in the sweltering heat for six hours waiting for a lift but instead drove north to St.Jean de Luz and sought out, not an old cream- coloured building with red shutters, but a modern establishment with an out-door swimming pool, which of course, Mary couldn't wait to jump into! The next morning, we set off on the long drive back up to Cherbourg and back to a future, which in its own way, was going to be another special journey.

15 ACTION.

"A ship is safe in harbour, but that is not what ships are for"

William Shedd.

Though Jim and I managed to sort out my anger-fuelled arguments, I was still angry with the whole psychiatric system in general and my own psychiatrist in particular. Unfortunately, he had now died. When I sought access to my records, the response said a lot. I had to pay a fee of E50 and they were supplied to me in a large, used envelope, a metaphor in itself for the way that particular individual had treated his patients. I could have let my anger consume me but thought it would be better to channel it into the movement, now emerging in Ireland, that was beginning to challenge the old orthodoxies of psychiatry.

And I wasn't the only one who was angry. In February 2002, Cork Advocacy Network had organised a second national conference in Jury's Hotel, Cork. Despite torrential rain and heavy flooding in the city, over 700 people packed the venue. The conference was chaired by Vincent Browne and Micheal Martin, Minister for Health, also attended. The anger in the hall was palpable with speaker after speaker severely critical of all aspects of the system - the budget cut-backs, the awful conditions of the hospitals, the over-reliance on medication, the ignoring of serious side-effects, the absence of alternative therapies and the general 'cinderella status' prevailing throughout. Personal story after personal story was told by people who felt the system had failed them. John McCarthy, of the white hair and long pony-tail, read his brilliant poem 'The Head'. It was my first time to meet the angry and passionate John. Normally nervous about speaking in public, I was inspired by the occasion to make my own contribution. It was a tremendous day and it was great to have been a part of it. I made many new friends and contacts as well as once again, meeting Terry Lynch who had been one of the main speakers and to whom I owed so much. Things were beginning to happen.

Building on the success of the conference, Joan Hamilton and C.A.N. now organised a series of monthly talks in The Commons Inn on the Mallow road. These were smaller and more intimate but most of all, they were informative and empowering. Woman of indefatigable energy that she is, Joan lined up speakers from home and abroad, all critical of the system. One of them was Paddy McGowan, a founder- member of The Irish Advocacy Network. Terry Lynch writes about him in his Book 'Beyond Prozac'.

"Paddy McGowan from Omagh, Co. Tyrone spoke of how, after three years of contact with psychiatry and the mental health services, he told a psychiatric nurse about the voices he had been hearing for years which to Paddy was as normal and familiar as the sun in the sky. The nurse sat up immediately, suddenly paying attention to every word. The next day his diagnosis was changed from post- traumatic stress (precipitated by the experiences of working as a fireman during the Troubles in Northern Ireland, having to deal with the aftermath of shootings and bombings) to schizophrenia and his whole life changed as a consequence. That happened in 1984 when he was twenty-three years old. It did not matter to the psychiatrists that he had heard voices for the previous fourteen years and that to him, they seemed entirely normal. Had the doctors explored the voices with him, they would have discovered that the voices began two weeks after the death of a much-loved relative. This surely pointed to a stress or grief reaction rather than evidence of a 'mental illness'.

"Paddy was immediately put on major tranquilizers. He remained on the medication for ten years. Eventually, he decided that he was getting nowhere on the medication. With the help of friends who were themselves familiar with the process of weaning oneself off medication, he gradually came off the drugs. His final prescription would have knocked out a horse: Largactil, a major tranquilizer, 1,600mgs daily (300mgs is the highest recommended daily dose); Depixol, another major tranquilizer, injection of 80mgs weekly; Prothiaden, an anti- depressant with sedative side-effects, 150mgs twice daily (twice the highest recommended daily dose of 150mgs). Ironically, the only thing not tranquilized by this concoction of medication was the sound of the voices for which he was put on the medication in the first place.

"Coming off the drugs in 1994 was a major struggle for Paddy but he got through it. Apart from the group of people who helped him to come off the medication, Paddy did not tell anyone that he was coming off the drugs. Over the years he had learnt that if he did tell people (including the psychiatrist), they would insist that he continue with his medication. For three years, Paddy found himself in a bizarre situation; he was off all medication but everyone around him thought he was continuing on the drugs as usual. Paddy's family and friends soon noticed big changes in him. They would often say that Paddy was 'himself' again. They marvelled at the wonders of modern medicine and in particular, Paddy's medication which was obviously now working effectively. Everyone was talking about the miraculous improvement in Paddy's condition. Paddy describes this as an 'internal prison'; he wanted to tell everyone that he was off medication and doing brilliantly without drugs but he could not tell anyone for fear of being persuaded (or even forced) to go back on his medication."

It was great to hear Paddy's story, to talk to him and to learn about the work he and others like Kieran Crowe were doing in The Irish Advocacy Network.

In the summer of 2002, I got a phone-call from Terry Lynch. A national conference organised by a newly-formed group called The Irish Mental Health Alliance was being planned for Tullamore in September. Terry asked me if I would be prepared to be one of the main speakers. I would tell my story as a 'survivor' of the system. Nervous and all as I would feel about doing so, my determination to contribute to the 'cause' led me to agree. Jim and I drove up to Tullamore the day before. I had made some notes and Jim had prepared a number of photographs to be used as over-heads which showed me before, during and after my time in the psychiatric world. The conference wasn't open to the public but rather the psychologist Asta Ghee, one of the chief organisers, had sent invitations to a wide range of people from various organisations who had a direct interest in the area. Once again, Vincent Browne was in the chair.

I was due to be the second speaker but to facilitate a psychiatrist who had to leave early, I was re-scheduled to the final slot just before lunch. I wonder did the audience notice the irony. Over 400 people listened as I told my story. It was great therapy for me. I was with people who knew and empathised with me. Afterwards, I was showered with expressions of support and congratulations from many of them. Also on the platform that day was the Australian Dorothy Rowe, a renowned psychologist and leading campaigner in the U.K. I must confess to never having heard of her before. She too was very warm in her congratulations and what she had to say to me was very encouraging. She also presented me with a signed copy of her best-selling book 'Beyond Fear'. In the preface she writes: "There have been a great many changes in ideas about mental distress (what psychiatrists call mental illness or mental disorder) and in the ways people suffering from mental distress are treated. However, many of the old ideas and old methods of treatment remain and there are still many people who are determined to resist change." There, she was setting out the challenge that faced all of us who were present that day in Tullamore. At the end of the day, I agreed to be nominated as one of the committee established to carry on the campaign.

That day in Tullamore, we were also given a booklist. Apart from 'Beyond Fear', I now acquired another book 'Users and Abusers of Psychiatry' by Lucy Johnson. Here was another person describing things, as I knew from my experience, to be absolutely true. "Many (patients) will be taking several (drugs) at once in potentially dangerous combinations or 'cocktails' - this is known as polypharmacy - or in very high doses …According to one survey, nearly one half of the patients who were on medication were taking two or more drugs…one third of the patients on major tranquilizers were taking two at once, by mouth and by slow release injection, despite evidence that this increases the risk of tardive dyskinesia." In 'Toxic Psychiatry', Peter Breggin speaks about tardive dyskinesia. "The term 'tardive' means late-developing or delayed; 'dyskinesia' means abnormal movement. Tardive dyskinesia is a movement disorder that can afflict any of the voluntary muscles, from the eyelids, tongue, larynx and diaphragm to the neck, arms, legs and torso. On rare occasions, it can occur after a few weeks or months but usually it strikes the individual after six months to two years of treatment." Another side-effect described in the same book is 'tardive akathesia' which is defined as "a permanent need to move about, accompanied by sometimes dreadful anxiety." I knew of that side-effect only too well.

Tullamore afforded me the opportunity of meeting many new people and establishing connections and contacts. To use a modern 'buzz' word, it was all about 'net- working'. At my age, I wasn't too familiar with 'buzz' words or the modern technology of computers but that same year, 2002, Claire and her boyfriend Tim had taken a year off to travel around the world. Before they left, they gave us a present of a PC with internet connection to enable us to keep in touch. While Jim had some experience of computers in school, I had absolutely none but I quickly picked it up.

It was amazing to enjoy the benefits of e-mails with Claire and Tim but the world of anti-psychiatry opened to me by the internet was even more exciting. Making full use of the Google search engine, I now entered a whole new realm, beyond the borders of Ireland, of yet more information and enlightenment. It was simultaneously uplifting and challenging - uplifting to discover just how well organised people were in other countries and the progress they were making and challenging to realise that here in Ireland, we have so much more to do.

It was at this stage that I encountered another remarkable man - Greg White. Greg is from Cobh. He had spent much of his life in southern Africa before returning to Ireland to practise as a psychotherapist in West Cork. Greg is an original thinker and true philosopher. He too had been present at the C.A.N. conferences in Cork. He had heard about me and was most anxious to explore with me the whole notion of 'recovery'. Being of a philosophical nature myself, we were both very much on the same wavelength. It was Greg who in turn told me of MindFreedom.org.

MindFreedom/Support Coalition International, to give it its full name, was established in 1990 in America by David Oaks. David is a survivor of the system himself. MindFreedom/SCI campaigns for human rights in the mental health system by uniting individual members and over one hundred grassroots sponsor groups. Every affiliated sponsor group has pledged itself to oppose forced psychiatric oppression and to promote empowering alternatives. For me, discovering this web-site was thrilling, exciting and eye-opening all at once. I was introduced to the e-mail list where I exchanged views with other survivors, not just from America but all over the world. These were my fellow sisters and brothers in suffering. I stood with them and they stood with me. It was a great feeling. We were on the move. I encountered for the first time the terrific battle cry 'Nothing about us without us'. I began to receive copies of the inspiring MindFreedom Journal. It was just so wonderful to read the articles, features and poems contributed by fellow survivors. I discovered the 'Mad Market' which is their wide-ranging stock of books and videos, a fantastic resource for all campaigners.

And it was this campaigning, particularly the active campaigning, that really impressed me. In Ireland, the cause is served mostly by conferences, newspaper articles, letter-writing, phone-ins and the occasional tv programme, all very worthwhile. But we have been shy when it comes to direct street protest. Not so the Americans. There, MindFreedom has been in the frontline of public protest, regularly picketing the annual meeting of the American Psychiatric Association with signs reading 'Psychiatrists cure Dissent not Disease' and 'No Forced Psychiatric Drugging'. As David Oaks himself puts it "We're calling for a non-violent, global revolution of self-determination and empowerment."

In August 2003, MindFreedom organised a public Hunger Strike outside the annual conference of the A.P.A. in Los Angeles. It threw down a challenge to the A.P.A. and the U.S. Surgeon -General to produce

*evidence that clearly establishes the validity of 'schizophrenia', 'depression' or other 'major mental illnesses' as biologically-based brain diseases

*evidence for a physical diagnostic examination such as a scan or test of the brain, blood, urine, genes etc. that can reliably distinguish individuals with these diagnoses (prior to treatment with psychiatric drugs) from individuals without these diagnoses

*evidence for a base-line standard of neurochemically balanced 'normal' personality against which a neurochemical 'imbalance' can be measured and corrected by pharmaceutical means

*evidence that psychotropic drugs can correct a 'chemical imbalance' attributed to psychiatric diagnosis and is anything more than a non-specific alterer of brain physiology

*evidence that any psychotropic drug can reliably decrease the likelihood of violence or suicide

*evidence that psychotropic drugs do not in fact increase the overall likelihood of violence or suicide.

These were exactly the questions I wanted to ask. I was delighted to see the psychiatric establishment being challenged in this way. I felt I had something to contribute to the cause. I had 'done my time'. I had seen the system from the inside. I knew how it worked. I was a survivor. I was going to fight!

Activism!

16 COMING OUT.

" Blessed are the cracked for they shall let in the light"

Unknown.

Silence and stigma feed off each other. This is especially true given the relatively small population we have in Ireland. There was a time when people were ashamed to admit they had TB. How many gay people lived lives of quiet desperation? It was only when people like Colm O'Gorman, the founder of the One-in-Four support group for victims of clerical sex abuse, spoke out that others were emboldened to come out with their own stories. Sadly today, words like 'psychiatric' and 'mental illness' still drip with stigma.

While I had spoken in public at this stage, it was a kind of 'sheltered' public, mostly fellow-sufferers as in C.A.N or Tullamore. But that day in Tullamore, I was also approached by Lydia Sapouna. Lydia is from Greece and works in the Department of Applied Social Studies in University College, Cork. As a result of our conversation, a few weeks later I found myself, along with Joan Hamilton, addressing a group of young social science students in the Old Lecture Hall. Claire and Sheena had both studied there for a time but little did I think then that I would be back speaking to students like them a few years later! Joan and I were very taken by our reception. We were asked lots of questions and we all found the exercise to be very worthwhile to such an extent that Lydia asked us to repeat it for a second group of mature students. We also spoke at the inaugural Mental Health Innovations One- Day Forum in U.C.C. organised by Lydia and Professor Fred Powell.

In a wider context, things were now beginning to happen. A new Mental

Health Act had been passed in 2001 though not yet fully implemented. The new act allowed for the setting up of The Mental Health Commission, which did come into being in April, 2002. In August 2003, The Expert Group on Mental Health Policy was established to prepare a national policy framework for the modernisation of the mental health services. The Expert Group held two consultation seminars and also invited submissions from the public, an invitation to which I was glad to respond. The Irish Advocacy Network also asked me to participate in a taped interview session which was part of their final submission to The Expert Group. I had been nominated to the Committee of C.A.N. in 2003 and was active on behalf of a friend. Part of my taped interview described what happened when I went to see my friend's psychiatrist: "In the beginning (on an earlier occasion) she didn't want to see me at all. Then the last time (subsequent visit) she wasn't going to see me again but I had the Amnesty book with me because in that they say that she (service user) has a right to have someone to speak for her ... and when I went in to see her with all this entourage around her ...she was making (service user) out to be a bully and she couldn't see that she was a bully herself the way she was treating her (service user)." It was empowering to stand up to such people.

The Amnesty book referred to was one of a series of booklets launched by the Irish branch of Amnesty International in the spring of 2003 to highlight the abuse of human rights which patients were still suffering in Irish psychiatric hospitals. In the Preface to 'Mental Illness - The Neglected Quarter', Sean Love, Director quotes Gabor Gombos, the Hungarian mental health rights activist "I remind myself that many of the mistakes in mental health care come from a helping attitude. But they want to help you without asking you, without understanding you, without involving you, in your best interest." On the question of stigma, the booklet quoted from The World Health Organisation Report for 2001. "Tackling stigma requires a multi-level approach involving education of health professionals and workers, the closing down of psychiatric institutions which serve to maintain and reinforce stigma, the provision of mental health services in the community and the implementation of legislation to protect the rights of the mentally ill."

At this stage I must state that I do not ever use the term 'mental illness' myself. It is a term which fits in with psychiatry's 'medical model'. I prefer the term 'emotional distress'. I agree with Peter Breggin, Terry Lynch, Dorothy Rowe and David Oaks when they say that psychiatry has never provided a blood test or any other test to prove the existence of 'mental illness' because no such test exists. In the foreword to Peter Breggin's 'Toxic Psychiatry', Dorothy Rowe says that we don't need psychiatrists who believe in the concept of 'mental illness'. "Anyone who has the necessary wisdom, sympathy and patience - a psychologist, a counsellor, a good friend - could give the help the sufferer needs."

To coincide with the launch of the Amnesty Report, TV3 approached my friend Helena and myself to appear on a special programme they were making called 'Out of Sight, Out of Mind'. Helena was in Carrigmor, the locked unit in Cork from where I sometimes took her out for the day. On the morning we were being filmed, I drove out to collect her. We told the staff she was coming to my house for lunch. I was apprehensive something would go wrong or that some of the nurses would find out the truth. We both had a sense of conspiratorial delight as we drove to the hotel to meet the TV crew. They then filmed me driving up the hill and into the driveway of my house. This had a special significance for me when I thought back to all the years I was crippled by drugs and found it so hard to drive. Now I was free and able to drive at my ease, even on film! John, the interviewer and his crew were very courteous and treated us with respect. We knew most of the filming would be edited as it was only a half-hour programme and other people were involved too, including Joan Hamilton. When it was shown, we were given about ten minutes but were pleased to have made our contribution to highlighting the human rights abuses in the system. A telling statistic came from Dr. John Owens, the newly appointed Chairman of The Mental Health Commission who said that 70% of admissions to mental hospitals were re-admissions. Clearly, something wasn't working. This was why Joan Hamilton had established Sli Eile to campaign for a therapeutic centre to which people would actually want to come. Sadly neither the programme nor the Amnesty Report received much follow-up in the media, coinciding as they did with the outbreak of the war in Iraq and the barbaric Operation 'Shock and Awe', though I know the video is being used for educational purposes in some universities and colleges.

However, I continued with my campaigning. I wrote letters to the newspapers, I spoke on radio, I read more and more books and I exchanged news and views with my contacts on the internet.

In November, 2003 Jim and I went to see the psychiatrist under whose care I was after my original and long-standing psychiatrist had died. I wanted to show him how I was now and tell him of my journey. He listened, but in a very condescending way. He had no time for Terry Lynch or his book and claimed never to have heard of Peter Breggin or MindFreedom. His attitude was 'Thank God you're great now but what does the future hold?' - a message of fear rather than encouragement. I asked him did he know what the future held for him and left, happy to have made my point.

Early in 2004, Jim and I decided to establish an Irish branch of MindFreedom. It was such a great organisation and I identified so much with it. Though I was also on the Committee of C.A.N., I saw the two organisations as complementary. The MindFreedom banner first appeared in public outside the Rochestown Park Hotel in Cork. Ireland held the E.U. Presidency at the time and inside, Micheal Martin was hosting a meeting of all the E.U. health ministers along with a special guest, Tommy Thompson, the U.S. Health Secretary. MindFreedom took its place alongside the other anti-war, anti-incinerator and pro-choice protestors. Later on, a delegation from MindFreedom had a meeting with Michael Martin on the issue of forced treatment. "Way to go!" was the response of David Oaks when we told him.

But my biggest 'coming out' was on the R.T.E. award-winning programme Prime Time Investigates. Reporter Eithne O'Donovan and producer Tara Peterman along with a film crew spent a whole day interviewing Jim and me. They also filmed me in the swimming pool where Alex, the Italian cameraman, showed his professionalism with some underwater shots! The programme was called 'Drug Money' and as Eithne explained, was about the companies that make the drugs, the doctors who prescribed them and the patients who take them. Altogether, four of us 'patients' spoke of our experiences - Kevin McPartlan of The Irish Advocacy Network bravely told of his attempted suicide, Evelyn Devine Millar spoke on the question of stigma, I spoke about the side-effects I experienced while on medication while Keelan spoke about the problems he encountered in trying to come off the drugs. Some startling statistics were given. Over E50 million was spent on over 300,000 prescriptions for anti-depressants in Ireland in 2002! Terry Lynch spoke of how G.P.s veered towards medication rather than counselling and of the need to use accurate language - 'adverse effects' rather than 'side effects' - when talking about drugs. An enlightened psychiatrist, Dr. Michael Corry said that G.P.s were given no training in counselling and only 3% of psychiatrists had a recognised qualification in psychotherapy. "If your only instrument is a hammer, everything is going to look like a nut" was the way he put it.

Jim also spoke about the hallucinations I experienced as an adverse effect of the Surmontil I was taking.

In an experiment carried out by Prime Time, a researcher presented himself to 15 doctors with only three of the minimum five symptoms that should be present for a diagnosis of depression, according to W.H.O. guidelines. These were i) a two month period of unhappiness, ii) an inability to enjoy every-day activities and iii) a lack of energy. Fourteen of the 15 doctors prescribed anti-depressant medication. When the experiment was repeated with the researcher presenting himself with just one symptom - feeling down - 9 out of the second 15 doctors prescribed medication. Dr. Dermot Walsh, the former Inspector of Mental Hospitals, admitted that despite the newer and supposedly better SSRI drugs, neither the number of admissions to, nor the length of stay in mental hospitals, had declined. Neither had the rate of suicide, which, on the contrary, as everybody knows, had actually increased. Part Two of the programme highlighted the huge profits being made by the drug companies - $36 billion by the top ten in the U.S. in 2002. Mention was made of the 3 Fs tactic they used to market their products to the doctors - Food, Flattery and Friendship. Despite Irish Medical Council guidelines about the educational content of sponsored trips and events, the impression was given that these were frequently breached. Dr. Tom O'Dowd, Professor of General Practice in Trinity College, didn't put a tooth in it when he spoke about 'bribery'. The programme concluded with a selection of quotes from the four of us 'patients'. I said "People say I'm great for getting up every morning to go to the pool but I just love it. I love getting up. Every morning I get up, it's terrific. I just love doing the things I could never do for all those years I was on drugs."

I received lots of positive feed-back after the programme. It was all part of helping to break the stigma but there was still a long way to go.

And, in a manner of speaking, the following month Jim and I did go a long way when we flew into Los Angeles for a holiday. We hired a car and spent a few weeks driving up the coast to San Francisco along Highway One. Before we left home, I had told David Oaks we were going to be in California and asked him were there any MindFreedom activists we could meet. In this way, we learned of a MindFreedom seminar in Berkeley which coincided with our stay, so we went along. It was on a Sunday afternoon in the community room of the Berkeley Main Library on Shattuck Avenue. The seminar, which was about electric shock, was one of a series being held over the summer entitled 'Critical Perspectives on

Psychiatry'. We were proud to announce ourselves as being from MindFreedom Ireland and make some valuable new contacts.

The main speaker that day was Ted Chabasinski who told his story. Ted was from a poor family where there were lots of problems and he had been removed by a social worker. At the age of SIX, he had received electroshock and had spent most of his childhood in the psychiatric system. Eventually discharged as a teenager, he became involved with an ex-patients' group in California from which he drew much support. He then went to college and qualified as an attorney and a patients' rights advocate. In 1982, the year I was in the psychiatric GF ward of the Regional Hospital in Cork, he set up a Berkeley Against Shock group and managed to have a local government vote passed which banned the use of electroshock in the local Herrick Hospital. Not surprisingly, The American Psychiatric Association gained a court order to have the ban overturned but for forty-one days, there had been no ECT administered in Herrick Hospital. It was the first time in the world that ECT had been banned, if only for a short time. Today, it is still being used in Cork and other Irish hospitals. As Ted recounted his story, many of his listeners were in tears. It was inspiring to listen to him and a privilege to speak to him afterwards.

He has been an inspiration to many others too including a woman called Judi Chamberlain who is a leading international campaigner in the survivor movement. In 'Toxic Psychiatry' Peter Breggin writes: "Chamberlain's personal exposure to psychiatry began in 1965 when she had a miscarriage. Twenty-one years old, unhappily married and a secretary without much of a future, the loss of the baby was one blow too many for her. She became depressed. Her first psychiatrist, she told me recently, turned out to be 'ineffectual and bland. I hardly remember what we talked about' What does an ineffectual, bland male psychiatrist do with a passionate, depressed but brilliant and attractive young woman who might somehow threaten him? He drugs her. A naïve youngster in those days, Chamberlain didn't know any better than to take the medication. She told me 'He was the expert. He was supposed to know. He said that the drugs were going to make me feel better, so he ought to know. I was very trusting.' When she only got worse, Chamberlain tried to admit herself to a private hospital. Its beds were full but instead of sending her home as she wished, the doctors whisked her off to the psychiatric ward of New York City's Bellevue Hospital. She arrived there, was held incommunicado and realised to her terror that no one in the world knew where she was. Among other things, they took away her glasses, leaving this frightened young woman nearly blind in her new environment. Petrified and brain-disabled by neuroleptics, Chamberlain became progressively more irrational.

She explained 'They took somebody who was going through a depression in reaction to losing her baby and made a 'schizophrenic' out of her.' She began to believe and even to see her face 'collapsing'. The bones were caving in on themselves, painfully, right in front of her eyes. But the 'delusions'and 'hallucinations' were filled with meaning. 'I was being de-humanised. Losing my face was a representation of what was happening to me. I was being turned into something else, something other than myself.'

Between March and October, 1966 Chamberlain was in six different hospitals. 'I'd become totally demoralised - like my life was over. I was told I was a chronic schizophrenic and would never be able to survive outside an institution.' She went home to live with her parents. At home Chamberlain happened to visit her internist, who referred her to a psychologist. 'He turned out to be a great guy - someone who built me up and made me feel there was no reason why I couldn't do anything I wanted to do.' When she told him that she had been diagnosed 'chronic schizophrenic, with no future,' he didn't buy it. Of the good qualities that this therapist displayed, it was his respect for her that mattered most. Chamberlain worked with him for about a year, at first in individual therapy and then in group as well. She's had no therapy since then.

Despite her successful therapy, Chamberlain still harboured profound doubts about herself. Why had she become 'mentally ill'? Why had she failed to benefit from all those treatments that were supposed to help? Then in 1971 she learned about the MPLP, the Mental Patients' Liberation Project in New York City. One of the first people she met was Ted Chabasinski. 'It was like a door opening.'

I could see so many parallels with my own story. She was a woman I would have loved to meet and two weeks later, amazingly purely by chance, I did - not in America but in the sportshall of a school in Denmark!!

17 DANISH DELIGHT.

*" The salvation of mankind is in the hands of the creatively
maladjusted"*

M.Luther King.

The school was the Vejle College of Sports. Vejle is a small town situated on a fiord on the eastern side of the Jutland peninsula. Between July 17 and 21, 2004 it was the venue for what was for me, an amazing event - an international congress on the theme of 'Networking for our Human Rights and Dignity' jointly organised by the World Network of Users and Survivors of Psychiatry (WNUSP) and the European Network of (ex-) Users and Survivors of Psychiatry (ENUSP). Coming from where I had over the previous four to five years, this was like being present at the 'Woodstock' of the international survivor movement. To use an American expression, it was awesome!

And, as I said, fortuitous circumstances got me the ticket. At a routine committee meeting of C.A.N. in early May, the chairman Kevin McPartlan asked if anyone was interested in accepting an invitation C.A.N. had received to attend a congress in Denmark in July. Kevin himself had other commitments and John McCarthy, who would have been the next person most likely to go, didn't happen to be present at our meeting that night. So I said I would be interested but that I would discuss it with Jim first as I would like him to accompany me and the invitation would not cover his travelling expenses. He was very enthusiastic when I told him and we proceeded to arrange our flights from Dublin to Copenhagen on the internet.

On receiving the full programme of events, talks and speakers, I was even more excited. Listed for delivering one of the three welcoming speeches at the official opening was Judi Chamberlain. Alongside her on the platform would be Gabor Gombos, the renowned Hungarian activist I was familiar with and, as I was to discover later, the dynamic and charismatic Karl Bach Jensen, the chief Danish organiser. I was also delighted that Peter Lehmann from Berlin, the ENUSP Secretary would be present. I knew he had just recently edited and published a book 'Coming Off Psychiatric Drugs', a collection of twenty-eight accounts from people around the world who had made the decision to withdraw from their drugs. I was most anxious to meet him and acquire a copy of the book.

So within two weeks of touching down in Ireland after our flight from San Francisco, Jim and I were taking off again on the morning Aer Lingus flight from Dublin and less than two hours later, were flying in over a sun-drenched Copenhagen harbour and its shining white wind farms. It was another two-hour train journey across the many islands and bridges of this part of Denmark before we eventually arrived in Vejle.

WNUSP grew out of users' and survivors' demands for recognition and represent- ation. In their joint press release, WNUSP describes itself as "an international disability organisation that seeks to improve the lives of people facing mental health difficulties by seeking alternative forms of recovery, fighting abuses within the psychiatric system and promoting a dialogue of reform among both health professionals and users and survivors of psychiatry." while ENUSP describes itself as "an initiative to give (ex-) users and survivors of psychiatric services a means to communicate, to exchange opinions, views and experiences in order to support each other in the personal, political and social struggle against expulsion, injustice and stigma in our respective countries. ENUSP is the only grassroots umbrella organisation on a European level that unifies national organisations of (ex-) users and survivors of psychiatry across the continent."

There was an exciting buzz about the college as we checked in for registration and received our name badges. Altogether, there were over two hundred delegates from a total of fifty-two countries. Also present from Ireland were Paddy McGowan, Kieran Crowe and Colette Nolan from The Irish Advocacy Network and Diarmuid Ring, a service user and member of The Mental Health Commission. Two of the first things I noticed were the number of white pianos about the place (which would be put to great use later) and outside, a magnificent heated swimming pool. What more could I ask?

Following the official opening and informal get-together on Saturday evening, the Congress got down to business on Sunday morning with a WNUSP general assembly. Delegates were invited from the floor to speak from the platform. Though nervous at the idea, I felt an unstoppable urge to take my place in the queue. When it came to my turn, I kept my speech short but let them know how thrilled and overjoyed I was to be present among them all and to experience the unbelievable atmosphere that had already been generated. The other point I made was to strongly state my opposition to the issue of forced treatment. The afternoon was given over to a series of regional meetings. All the proceedings were recorded by the Norwegian film-makers Hakon Sandoy and Askill Brunvoll. Two of their shocking videos, 'Force Against Conviction' and 'For Your Own Good', which have been shown on Scandinavian TV, were screened that night after dinner. They had a powerful effect on everybody, especially the latter, with its depiction of a lobotomy being carried out in a modern Norwegian hospital.

But it wasn't all serious. A bar had been installed in the college and a very convivial atmosphere prevailed in the evenings. Of course I was soon talking to Judi Chamberlin and swopping news and views. I also spoke with Peter Lehmann who presented me with a copy of his book, on condition that I wrote a review afterwards. Judi had written one of the three prefaces to the book: "Much of the conventional wisdom about psychiatric drugs is wrong. Psychiatrists and the pharmaceutical industry have successfully convinced much of the public, through the media, that psychiatric drugs are 'safe' and 'effective' in 'treating' 'mental illness'. How is it that these myths have been so successfully accepted as fact? For one thing, those promoting the drugs are authority figures, doctors and scientists who are generally accepted to be presenting value-free experimental results. Another factor, perhaps even more significant, is that those who are given the drugs and who are the ones who have spoken out about their negative effects are automatically discredited by having been labelled 'mentally ill'. The diagnosis of 'mental illness' carries with it a host of associations, particularly that the person so labelled has impaired judgement and ... is not a reliable reporter of his or her own experiences.

"Unfortunately, the media image of a person who has stopped taking psychiatric drugs is the one that has captured the popular imagination: a person so deluded that he or she is unable to realize that his or her behaviour is abnormal and who then usually goes on to commit some horrendous violent crime. Reading about real people (as in the book) and the complex reasons behind their decisions might be a way to counter this negative and destructive image.

"It is often said that psychiatric drugs are given to people labelled 'mentally ill' in order that those around them, such as medical personnel and family members, can feel better. Certainly, being around people who are troubled, especially when they are vocal about what is troubling them, can be wearing and difficult. But simply silencing them is not the answer. Instead, we need to listen carefully to the real experiences that people have so that we can learn the true costs of psychiatric drugs on people's lives."

One of the other prefaces was written by Loren Mosher, a father-figure of the anti-psychiatry movement. I had read a lot about him and his famous Soteria House project. Like Peter Breggin, he was a psychiatrist who had the backbone to stand up publicly and criticise his own profession. For his actions, very much like Terry Lynch in Ireland, he was widely ostracised. With Alma Menn they had established Soteria House (Soteria is the Greek word for Deliverence) in a rambling, two-storey wooden building in San Jose, California in 1971 which they adapted to accommodate six people diagnosed as 'schizophrenic'. Two full-time staff members plus various volunteers and part-time assistants would live with them and a house doctor and psychiatrist would contribute advice. Staff and residents did the cooking and other household chores and in the words of Loren, the staff "aimed to provide a simple, home-like, safe, warm, supportive, unhurried, tolerant and non-intrusive environ-ment." The project was very successful but because it was unconventional, those with the purse strings slowly cut off the funding. Loren explained "It had questioned so many of the psychiatric beliefs that people hold near and dear to their heart. Like that you need hospitals. That you need a trained staff. That you need neuroleptics. And that you need the medical model to explain things."

Soteria House eventually closed in 1983. Loren Mosher had continued his work in various reforming, Soteria-like projects around America but from the mid-80's, was becoming more and more concerned about the cosy relationship between The American Psychiatric Association and the pharmaceutical companies. Ultimately, he resigned from that body in 1998. His letter of resignation has become a manifesto of the survivor movement. "At this point in history, in my view, psychiatry has been almost completely bought out by the drug companies...Psychiatric training reflects (the Pharmaceutical industry's) influence as well: the most important part of a resident's curriculum is the art and quasi-science of dealing drugs, i.e. prescription writing...No longer do we seek to understand whole persons in their social contexts. .. Rather we are there to realign our patients' neurotransmitters. .. 'Biologically based brain diseases' are certainly convenient for families and practitioners alike. It is no-fault insurance against personal responsibility. We are all just helplessly caught up in a swirl of brain pathology for which no one, except DNA, is responsible." Declaring that he wanted "no part of a psychiatry of oppression and social control," Loren concluded by asking "Is psychiatry a hoax - as practiced today? Unfortunately, the answer is mostly yes."

In the preface to 'Coming Off Psychiatric Drugs', Loren speaks of us as living in an era of a 'pill for every ill'. "The focus of this book - the stories of people who were not listened to as they suffered torment of the soul, self and mind from psychiatric drugs, often given against their will, is very important. ...Because the drugs were given thoughtlessly, paternalistically and often unnecessarily to fix an unidentifiable 'illness', the book is an indictment of physicians. The Hippocratic Oath - to above all do no harm - was regularly disregarded in the rush to 'do something'. How is it possible to determine whether soul murder might be occurring without reports of patients' experiences with drugs that are aimed directly at the essence of their humanity? Despite their behaviour, doctors are only MDs not MDeitys. They, unlike gods, have to be held accountable for their actions."

Sadly, Loren Mosher died on Saturday, July 9th, 2004 - just a week before the Vejle Congress - in the Havelhoehe Clinic in Berlin where he had gone for treatment of a bad liver disease. It was with a deep sense of respect, gratitude and homage that I proposed to the final general assembly of the congress that we stand in silence to his memory.

Fittingly, it was from Berlin that another woman who greatly impressed me, came. She was Iris Holling who chaired many of the sessions. Iris is closely associated with The Runaway House project in Berlin which is a crisis centre for homeless survivors of psychiatry. Now in its twelfth year, the project is modelled on the Soteria House experience.

On Monday morning, there were speeches from Tina Minkowitz, U.S.A. on the U.N. Conventionon Human Rights and Dignity and the specific issue of forced treatment. Moosa Salie from South Africa spoke about Networking for Human Rights and Dignity from an African perspective while Liz Sayce, U.K. delivered a paper 'From Psychiatric Patient to Citizen - Overcoming Discrimination and Social Exclusion.'

In the afternoon we could choose to attend any one of twelve workshops.

I opted for 'The medical model - what's wrong with it - how can we counteract the globalisation of the medical model.' It was facilitated by Maths Jesperson from Sweden, who was spending part of his honeymoon at the congress! He is also the Regional secretary of the Swedish National Association for Social and Mental Health which runs the Hotel Magnus Stenbock in Helsingborg, another Soteria inspired project.

A concert was arranged for Monday night and everybody was welcome to contribute. I played a few tunes on the piano while the African delegates put on a fantastic display of dancing so infectious, it practically got the whole audience up on stage. Then there was music from a Danish survivors' band called Shock Rock, who were meant to be the final act. However, an impromtu Irish ballad session and singsong soon commenced around the piano and went on to a late hour.

On Tuesday there was a lot of tiring but necessary elections to boards and regional bodies. Colette Nolan was elected to the Board of ENUSP and I was nominated as a Deputy-member. Later I was interviewed on film by Hakon Sandoy for the new video he and Askill were making on survivors while he also filmed me playing the piano. I think he had been impressed by the ballad session!

I met and talked with users and survivors from everywhere - Australia, Brazil, France, Ghana, Holland, Israel, Japan, Malta, New Zealand, Nigeria, Russia, Switzerland and Zambia. Some were well recovered, others struggling along that road. One of these was Shewaye Berhanu from Ethiopia who was to become a particular friend. Shewaye is a lovely girl with a flashing white smile and beautiful, braided hair. I happened to sit by her one day at lunch. I had never met anyone from Ethiopia before. She told me her story, how she had been diagnosed with 'bi-polar mood disorder' and was still taking medication. She was the same age as my daughter Claire and was at a stage where I had once been myself, which made me especially connect with her. We went swimming together every morning before breakfast and I showed her how to float and relax. We also played the piano together and did a lot of dancing which she really liked. I promised to send her a copy of 'Beyond Prozac' when I got home and we have been in regular contact ever since. She is making good progress in her studies and the future is promising.

There was a Farewell Dinner and party on Tuesday night and on Wednesday morning, it was goodbyes all round. It had been an unforgettable few days, taxing and intense at times, but ultimately inspiring and rewarding. I would like to pay a special tribute to Karl Bach Jensen, the main Danish organiser. His passion and commitment shone out like a beacon. He was a source of energy from which we were all able to charge our batteries to sustain us for the road ahead.

Jim and I travelled back to Copenhagen where we were glad to relax for a few days strolling around Nyhaven and the Tivoli Gardens, sampling the delights of the pastry shops, not to mention 'probably the best lager in the world'!

Denmark was an important milestone in my journey of recovery. I was learning all the time, making contacts and feeling great to be part of a movement that was on the march. I value my name-badge from Vejle as I would a campaign medal. Thanks to C.A.N., I had had the good fortune of meeting many of the vanguards of that march in Denmark. Soon, I would meet more of them in back in Ireland.

With Shewaye from Ethiopia

18 STOP, STOP, STOP.

"Be the change you want to see in the world."

Gandhi.

One of the first things I did when I came home was to read 'Coming off Psychiatric Drugs' and write my review for Peter Lehmann who subsequently posted it on the internet. I also arranged to meet Terry Lynch. Over the years, we had kept in regular touch. Terry was always a tremendous support and would often text me with news of any developments or articles he had come across. I had picked up an array of literature in Denmark in which I knew he would be interested. I also had a second copy of Peter's book to give him. Because of the stand he has taken, Terry's road can be an isolated one so I thought all the news from Denmark would be a morale boost for him too, which indeed it was. Jim and I met him in Charleville. At the time, we didn't realise how familiar with the town we were later to become.

Another great woman I had met since my campaigning involvement was Orla 0' Donovan who was a colleague of Lydia Sapouna in the Department of Applied Social Studies in U.C.C. In September 2004, Orla, along with Kathy Glavanis-Grantham from the Department of Sociology, organised a two-day conference entitled 'Health, Democracy and the Globalised Pharmaceutical Industry - Exploring the Politics of Drug Regulation Internationally and in Ireland.' As they stated in their publicity literature "Little discussion of these issues has taken place in Ireland, in spite of the intense dependency of the Irish economy on the globalised pharmaceutical industry." A comprehensive list of speakers had been lined up from home and abroad. Among the former was Terry Lynch who would speak on the dominance of drug-based approaches to mental health in Ireland. Orla asked me would I deliver a brief introductory talk for him, which of course

I was honoured to do. To coincide with the conference, the Irish Examiner featured an interview with me in which I gave a synopsis of my story and spoke of the help I had received from Terry and his book. They accompanied it with a large photo of our pet cat Ollie and me in our back garden. Introducing Terry at the conference I said "After a long struggle and much soul-searching, I realised that the drugs were killing my body and spirit. I had to get them out of my system. I did this slowly and fearfully. I always thought 'they' might be right and the psychiatric hospital- my hell- would be waiting for me.

It was at this point after my 50th birthday that I read 'Beyond Prozac' and later met Terry Lynch. Now there was someone from the medical profession saying the same things that I felt from my life experience. It was just the right time for me. Who he is and what he says has helped me in a huge way to be the person I am today - free of all drugs and more important, free to be myself, free to enjoy life." One of the overseas speakers on the controversy surrounding Seroxat was Charles Medawar, another respected campaigner and joint author along with Anita Hardon of 'Medicines Out of Control? - Antidepressants and the Conspiracy of Goodwill.' In Chapter One they explain that "this book tells a story that reveals some of the workings of medics and medicine and their impact on personal, community and global health ... The action runs from the mid nineteenth century to the foreseeable future. Over the years, the drugs in the story change and different ideas and actors hold sway. But the same patterns of behaviour emerge and the outcome is much the same. Users constantly emerge as losers - by no means universally, but always on a grand scale." Again, I was honoured to receive a copy from the author on which he had written 'To Mary - fighting and winning the good fight. With best wishes from Charles, Cork, September, 2004.' We all like a little pat on the back occasionally and I didn't even have to write a review!

In a paper entitled 'A Pathological Partnership? The Irish State and the Globalised Pharmaceutical Industry', Orla herself gave some pertinent facts about the Irish Medicines Board which oversees and regulates the safety of drugs in Ireland. "Only six of their one hundred staff have responsibility for pharmacovigilance- checking reported drugs that have had an adverse reaction." The IMB. is financed by the pharmaceutical industry and its first chairman was a chief executive of the Irish Pharmaceutical Healthcare Association. It was government policy to make the country attractive to the pharmaceutical industry. Further interesting information on that industry, specifically in the Cork region, was provided by Kathy Glavanis-

Grantham. Ireland is the biggest exporter of pharmaceuticals in the world. These exports were worth E33 billion in 2003 - 36% of our total exports. Nineteen of the seventy-two pharmaceutical plants are located in Cork, the majority American. Cork had become a comfort zone for the industry and the relationship between the University and the business was one of mutuality. "There is an unholy alliance between the universities, industry and the State and the government is the facilitator in this neo-liberal agenda". U.C.C. had developed a corporate ethos that sees students as clients of the pharmaceutical industry, she concluded. The conference was another eye-opener for me. These were more facts the public needed to know and the more the public knew, the better. It was to play our bit in informing the public that Jim and I agreed, when approached by Greg White on behalf of the Cork Aquarian Society, to give a public talk at the end of November, 2004. Entitled 'Thou Shalt Not Be Aware - a Cork Couple's Harrowing Experience of the Psychiatric Establishment', the talk attracted an audience of approximately one hundred to the Maryborough Hotel. For me it was another empowering exercise. It was great to have Jim up there with me and giving his perspective. The audience response was very encouraging and once again, many stories were told by people unhappy with the way they had been treated by the psychiatric establishment.

A few nights later in the Metropole Hotel, we saw that establishment at work. A public lecture called 'Mind Yourself - Overcoming Depression' was given by one of the country's best known psychiatrists, Professor Patricia Casey of U.C.D. and the Mater Hospital. On the subject of antidepressant medication, the following information was imparted. "Many side-effects will wear off after the first couple of weeks once your body gets used to the drug ... Some people worry that they may become addicted to their antidepressant. These drugs are not addictive. However, some people may experience discontinuation symptoms if they suddenly stop taking the drug." Not surprisingly, the lecture series, which was touring the country, was sponsored by Lundbeck (Ireland) Ltd., a leading pharmaceutical company.

I am proud to say that not one cent of 'pharmaceutical money' went towards another major conference organised by C.A.N. in February 2005. This conference was the culmination of months of effort and hard work by the new C.A.N. committee which had been elected in early November, 2004. The members of this committee were Rick Deedy, Eilis Foley, Helena King, Joe Maguire, Bart Murphy, Brendan O'Callaghan, John

O'Flynn and Mary O'Mahony. In addition, Rose Hannon was Treasurer, John McCarthy, P.R.O., Greg White, Chairman and I was Secretary. The planning had started right away. Contact was made with Lydia Sapouna and Professor Fred Powell of the Department of Applied Social Studies in U.C.C. who agreed to help. A venue, the Devere Hall in the Student Union Building, was acquired. As P.R.O., John McCarthy had lots of contacts. He was also a user-member of the Southern Health Board's Implementation Body, Focusing Minds. Among the speakers lined up were Tim O'Malley T.D, the junior Health Minister with specific responsibility for mental health, Dr. John Owens, Consultant Psychiatrist and Chairperson of the Mental Health Commission and Diarmuid Ring, a user representative on the Commission. Dr. Tony Bates, Psychologist in St. James' Hospital and member of the Expert Group, would be Chairperson.

After much discussion, we agreed on our conference title - 'Dignity - A Step to Recovery in 'Mental' Illness.' It was agreed that the main emphasis would be on the voice of the user/survivor. John McCarthy himself would speak but we also needed some international speakers to raise the profile of the conference. It was then that my contacts from the Denmark conference were useful as we were able to recruit two other survivors, Rowland Urey from the U.K. and Hannelore Klafki from Germany. For our main guest overseas speaker, we originally had in mind Dr. 'Patch' Adams from the U.S.A. but circumstances ruled him out, at which point I suggested we approach David Oaks, Director of MindFreedom. As I was in regular e-mail contact with him at this stage, I was assigned the job of getting him to come all the way from Oregon on the West Coast of America for a one-day conference in Cork. No matter, given my huge admiration for the man, I could think of no better task I would have been delighted to undertake.

Since I had been first introduced to MindFreedom, David Oaks had been an inspiration to me. Born on the South-Side of Chicago, he had won a Teamster's Union Scholarship to Harvard in 1973. Feeling uncomfortable among his privileged fellow students, he had experimented with marijuana. As he explains in his own words on the MindFreedom website: he "stopped sleeping ... For whatever reason, I had been entering altered states that were sometimes delightful, sometimes painful, but that all had some validity to my life - just as dreams often do ... There were times I thought a UFO was appearing in my living room or that God was talking to me via the radio." Altogether during his college years, he was hospitalised five times and diagnosed as a 'schizophrenic'. "I was told I would have to stay on psychiatric drugs for the rest of my life, like a diabetic on insulin. I was told I was genetically flawed and had a permanently broken brain." He was forcibly injected and locked in solitary confinement. "It was like taking a wrecking-ball to the cathedral of thoughts, feelings and experiences that defined me at that moment." Eventually discharged, David discovered the Boston-based Mental Patients Liberation Front where he learned the benefits of peer support, exercise and a healthy diet. He became more and more active with support and recovery groups, organising protests against the American Psychiatric Association and campaigning against the use of electro-convulsive therapy. In 1990, he established MindFreedom/Support Coalition International. "The fact that the movement has survived is due in large part to David's ability to work like a dog for almost no money" said Loren Mosher.

And that was exactly the generous spirit he displayed when I told him about our conference. Apart from covering his flight and modest accommodation, our only other outlay was a very reasonable fee. As the conference coincided with Valentine's Day, Debra, his wife, suggested they celebrate it together (she at her own expense) in Ireland, a place neither of them had previously visited. I was then able to offer them the use of my six-year old Punto for their few days of sight-seeing after the conference, which they greatly appreciated.

The conference was scheduled for Friday, February 11th. The committee organised some advance publicity. John McCarthy and I, along with Diarmuid Ring, did an interview with Valerie Fox for the Pat Kenny Radio Show while Pat also spoke to Tony Bates. Further feature articles appeared in the Irish Examiner and Susan Calnan wrote a full-page piece in the Health Supplement of the Irish Times. She quoted Greg White who put the conference in context "People - patients, carers and medics alike - didn't, nor do they now, want to believe that 'mental illness' is a skewed medico-social construct which ignores the shocking perceptions of a small but growing number of individuals who have got through it and come out the other side." On the specific conference theme of 'Dignity', I was quoted: "To me, the most important thing is that people with mental health problems are given a choice and a say in their own treatment; so that if a person is put on medication, that it's their decision and not somebody else's. But there should also be a much greater emphasis put on the simple things that people can do for themselves - diet, exercise, music, proper sleep, relaxation - to help them in their recovery. I feel that my life was taken away from me for twenty years and although I sometimes feel angry about that, I want to channel this energy into helping other people through their recovery and to help them realise that there are different ways and not just one way, of overcoming the pain they may be experiencing in their lives at that time."

Understandably, I was very excited as I drove up to Cork Airport on the afternoon of Thursday, February 10th, 2005. I was going to meet one of my new-found heroes. I had organised a few of our MindFreedom, Ireland members to be on hand to welcome David and Debra. Martin, Eileen, Maria, Helena, John and Jim were all there waiting, complete with a huge MindFreedom banner that Bridget Daly, the art teacher in Jim's school, had especially made for the occasion. Apart from John who had seen a photo somewhere, none of us knew what David looked like other than that he had a beard. However, our MindFreedom banner stood out like a beacon and instantly caught the attention of the casually-dressed, long-haired, bespectacled David. Helena presented Debra with a piece of Stephen Pearce pottery, hugs and kisses were exchanged, photographs taken and then we all adjourned to the Great Southern Hotel for some welcoming pints of Murphy's. Despite their long flight from Oregon, both were in great form. Tempting as it was to settle in for the evening, we didn't want David burdened with a hangover next morning so after an hour or so, John McCarthy drove them to their guesthouse on the Western Road.

Jim and I stayed on to collect Rowland Urey and his wife who were arriving from Manchester. We had met them in Denmark. They were staying in the same guesthouse as David and Debra and after dropping them off, it was back up to the airport to meet Hannelore Klafki who was arriving from Berlin. Hannelore was only staying two nights and was very anxious to visit an Irish pub so we accompanied her to the Wine Vaults near the university where she too sampled the local brew and adapted to our local smoking conventions.

This was the third major C.A.N. conference and like the others, drew a capacity audience of more than four hundred. Users and survivors would be given a platform to speak while the politicians and professionals, aside from their own contributions, would primarily be there to listen. Diarmuid Ring was not going to accept any discrimination. "It beggars belief that we still have no service user on the Mental Health Inspectorate. I will not rest until I see a service-user with the same parity of esteem and parity of income as any professional assistant inspector." In a passionate and powerful contribution, John McCarthy said it was time for us to say 'Stop' - stop treating us like you have, stop talking down to us, stop ignoring us.

We have an 'expertise' which needs to be listened to. He challenged Dr. Owens to "let us be our own advocates and speak with our own voice" and concluded by inviting the audience to repeatedly shout out loudly and clearly ' Stop, Stop. Stop'.

It was a defining moment of the conference. Hannelore Klafki is a founder-member of the German Hearing Voices Network. Her message to the professionals echoed John's. Voice-hearers have an 'experience expertise' which should be listened to. The content of the voices needs to be examined, not suppressed by drugs. It is very disempowering to be told to accept that your experience of voices is not relevant. Hannelore wanted to tell the professionals that the key to understanding the voices lies within the content of the voices. The professionals need to learn and speak a new language that both they and the users understand. Founder-member of the Oldham Mental Health Forum, Rowland Urey, with his own inimitable Mancunian humour, said a paradigm shift in mental health care was needed. The professionals definition of CARE was to 'Cover Arse to Retain Employment'. Our definition of care was to create alternative recovery environments and he asked the professionals to join us in that task.

While Tony Bates was the general chairperson for the day, I was asked, because of my previous contact with them, to introduce the overseas speakers. I was glad to avail of the opportunity to put across a few points to the professionals. The 'medical model' was failing I said, because it used 'external control' or 'domination' as David Oaks himself was to say later. For me, being part of MindFreedom and ENUSP was invigorating and empowering, being part of the psychiatric system was self-destructive and dis-empowering, leaving people, as my good friend Helena says, "helpless and hopeless". It was a privilege and an honour for me to introduce Hannelore, Rowland and Mr. MindFreedom himself, the now smartly suited David Oaks. David's message for the professionals was that we were not calling for reform but for a non-violent revolution. The general public too had to be warned that a "tsunami of human rights violations" was spreading across the world. Mental health treatment should be about choice. If some people wanted to take drugs, we must respect their decision but equally, people must not be forced to take them. He used the analogy of someone being forced to take a pint of Murphy's twice a day. This was what he called the 'domination model' and it violated our human rights. The public also has to be told that psychiatry's 'chemical imbalance theory' has never been proven. "There was no lab-test, no urine test, no genetic screening, no more proof for it than for astrology or tarot". Long-term use of neuroleptic drugs can cause brain damage so severe that it shows up on scans. It led to "frontal-lobe shrinkage" which put it in the same category as psycho-surgery and lobotomy. Again, he stressed to the professionals that "forced long-term use of neuroleptics is an extreme violation of human rights". The voices of users/survivors must be listened to and acted upon and he concluded with the battle-cry 'Nothing about us without us'.

For the Mental Health Commission, Dr. John Owens accepted that there was much that was wrong in the current system. "It is good in parts, there are a lot of committed, well-trained people but many are demoralised and burnt out." He admitted that the people who provide services in the past "have not listened that well". He had high hopes for the upcoming Report from the Expert Group which would "turn things upside down". He promised that the Mental Health Commission would look after the rights of patients and would be "fearless" in doing its job. Supporting Dr. Owens, Tim O'Malley said he wanted to challenge the whole system. "With your help, and I emphasise your help, I want to change things. There are vested interests who are against change. We have knocked down the old walls but we must now knock minds." He was glad to see the conference focusing on "something dear to my heart - the recovery model of mental health." Tony Bates explained how things work. "What you say becomes part of the conversations that very key people have who are the service providers and those conversations shape debate and very often, ideas that have been held to be sacred are challenged and toppled ... so what you say becomes the printed word and the printed word becomes policy and policy shapes the way services are developed." The professionals, he said, were actually persuaded by arguments that people make that are reasonable and heartfelt. These were all fine words coming from Tim O'Malley, Dr. Owens and Dr. Bates but the big question was would they be really matched by fine action. Time would tell. In the wonderful general discussion and debate that followed the speeches, the three men heard many more stories of pain, anger and disillusionment before the conference eventually concluded with a mass singing of 'We Shall Overcome'.

For everybody I think and certainly for me, it had been a terrific day. Many more people were becoming active and energising one another. The day had been another big step in the non-violent revolution. It was as

David Oaks said 'exhilarating' to be part of it and for me, a privilege to have been able to contribute to it as much as I had. The euphoric mood continued at the post-conference dinner attended by the guest speakers and the organising committee but two nights later, Jim and I had the opportunity to reflect on events in a more subdued atmosphere and in a manner which was a perfect conclusion to what had been a few hectic days.

The week following the conference was the school mid-term break and early in January, we had booked a short stay in the Woodlands Hotel in Adare. It had what looked from the brochure, a nice leisure centre for me and for Jim, a nearby golf course. We were delighted then when David Oaks told us that Debra, without knowing we were going to be there, had also booked accommodation for one night in Adare as part of their post-conference mini-tour of the southwest! Being so close to Limerick, I thought it was a great chance for David to meet Terry Lynch, who had been unable to attend the conference. I knew they would have a lot to say to each other. They certainly had but it wasn't all 'shop talk' as the five of us had dinner that Sunday night in the Woodlands. We all got to know one another on a more personal level and the talk was wide-ranging and light-hearted. For Jim and me, it was a very special evening to share the company of two such outstanding and courageous men, two, though they would never use the term themselves, of the 'generals' of the campaign.

And that campaign would continue on a number of other fronts in the future. As Jim and I drove back to Cork two days later, we stopped off to look at a house which had been purchased by Joan Hamilton and Sli Eile in Charleville. A few minutes later, we were being questioned by a member of An Garda Siochana who had followed us as we drove out of the town.

With Terry, David and Debra

19 DARKNESS AND LIGHT.

"We must accept finite disappointment, but we must never lose infinite hope"

Luther King.

Sli Eile evolved from C.A.N. and was founded by Joan Hamilton in 2002. One startling fact of the conventional psychiatric system is that 70% of admissions to mental hospitals are re-admissions. Progressive thinking suggested that there should be 'another way' - a Sli Eile. The government's own 'Health Strategy 2001 - Quality and Fairness' expressed "concerns about using only the traditional medical model of care for mental illness". The Southern Health Board's 'Focusing Minds' document also spoke about the "need to provide facilities where individuals can develop and practice living skills in a supported environment."

Joan is a tireless worker. I had got to know her over the years with my own involvement in C.A.N. where she had been a powerful driving force. When she asked Jim and myself to attend a public meeting to speak in support of a new project - a Sli Eile house in Rathcormac, just south of Fermoy - we were glad to be able to support her. Unfortunately, the building identified for the project proved unsuitable but, typical of her energy and will, Joan continued her quest.

Another house at Pike Farm in Charleville was found and as Sli Eile is a housing association with charitable status, it qualified for capital funding from the Department of the Environment. Regretably, in a move that was to create many problems, the news of the capital funding was announced in the local paper, The Vale Star, by an enthusiastic politician before Sli Eile had approached the residents of Pike Farm to inform them of the project and what precisely it involved.

Pike Farm is a small estate of eleven bungalows. The residents of Pike Farm are the same as residents anywhere in Ireland. Mention the words 'mental' or 'psychiatric' and the fear and stigma which surround those words immediately comes to the surface. People are afraid. They are afraid for their children. They are afraid for the property value of their houses. The only way such fears can be allayed is through knowledge and information and sometimes, even with that, the fear remains.

Hostile placards and signs soon appeared at the entrance to the estate stating that Sli Eile was not welcome. Early attempts to arrange a meeting between both sides foundered. Sli Eile produced a prospectus on the project which was made available to all concerned. It first of all set out the rationale for the house under the heading Community as Method. "The past decade has witnessed increased demand for alternatives to the medical treatment model of psychiatric care. During the past fifty years, a variety of alternative, supportive environments have been developed and evaluated in different parts of the world. The concept of community living is used to support people with long-term mental health and social problems to gain self-esteem and confidence in their ability to take charge of their lives." Acknowledging the influence of Loren Mosher and his Soteria House, the prospectus outlined the ethos of community living, explaining how the setting would be in keeping with other houses in the local community and would encourage interaction within it. It would be home-like and comfortable with participation on an informal and individualised basis. In addition, Sli Eile would encourage tenants to avail of all health and social services that were available to them. "In particular, Sli Eile hopes to continue building a good relationship with the North Cork Mental Health Team in relation to the identification of potential tenants and the utilisation of professional services that can only enhance the success of the project."

To me and from my experience of the psychiatric system, this was a great project. Joan asked me to join the Board but as I was very busy as secretary of C.A.N. at the time, I had to decline though I did become a member of the Project Support Group and Jim joined the Board. I would have loved to have spoken to the Pike Farm residents and let them see what a user/survivor was like. I didn't have horns, I was just an ordinary human being like themselves and their families. Anybody can experience emotional distress. But I didn't get a chance. A number of public meetings were called but the residents did not attend and the gulf between them and Sli Eile only widened.

It was a measure of the fear and discrimination prevalent today that such a small project could provoke such a big reaction. The house would cater for a maximum of five residents. As the prospectus said "The small number living in this particular house facilitates its operating structures to be determined and governed by those who live there. Carefully chosen and trained non-psychiatric staff are constantly on hand to provide a simple, safe, warm and cheerful environment. Sli Eile believes that sincere understanding and genuine respect for individual difference is crucial to healing interactions, which are person centered. Sli Eile provides psychological support to people who have been or still are being prescribed medication by their psychiatrist or G.P. These treatments are regarded as a personal matter for each individual tenant. The setting within the house is one where the tenant is not viewed as 'sick' nor is any discussion of diagnoses or labels encouraged, unless initiated by a tenant, as a matter of concern for himself or herself."

Yes, in an Irish context, there were aspects that were innovative but to me and others who supported Sli Eile, this was precisely what was needed. Sadly though, the local residents didn't want to know and began to employ tactics which in effect amounted to intimidation and harassment. Being stopped and questioned by the guard that day occurred because Jim and I had driven into Pike Farm to see the house and Jim had taken a few photographs of the protest signs. Obviously our presence was reported to the guards who were then obliged to follow up on it. Had we been acting suspiciously? Apparently, we were strangers taking photographs and had to be checked out!

But worse was to follow. As Sli Eile moved into the house and began to get it ready for its future use, the residents mounted a very intimidating 'silent' protest outside. Carrying placards reading 'Sli Eile Not Welcome' and 'Get out Stay Out', they paraded in front of the house and also erected placards on the back garden fence. Any attempt at dialogue or friendly greeting on our part was met with stoney silence. For a few weekends, a single service-user along with some Sli Eile volunteers, including Jim and myself, remained overnight in the house. If we left to go for a walk into town, we were accompanied at very close quarters by the protestors and their placards and subjected to more of the 'silent treatment'. One of the saddest aspects of the protest was to see the inclusion of teenagers and children. One of the houses in Pike Farm is occupied by St. Joseph's Foundation which helps people with a mental disability but the goodwill of the residents in that case apparently could not be extended to include Sli Eile. The events made headlines in the national press and on R.T.E. True, because of circumstances, it could be said that what upset the residents most was that they had not been approached by Sli Eile in the first instance and this severely damaged the vital bond of trust required for the project but the suspicion must remain - did that give them a convenient excuse? Ultimately though, the case outlined the major task in overcoming stigma still faced by campaigners, whether in Charleville or anywhere else in Ireland.

Fighting another aspect of that campaign in which I had a special interest was Nuria O'Mahony. Nuria is from Spain but was married to Niall and living with their three small children in Bandon. Nuria is a nurse who works in the A&E department in Cork University Hospital while Niall had worked as a psychiatric nurse tutor. I had first met Nuria at the conference on the pharmaceutical industry in U.C.C. in September, 2004. She had spoken from the audience that day about the need for the government to strengthen the regulatory framework for prescription drugs in Ireland. The reason why she was so concerned was that the previous December, her husband Niall had died from suicide in the garden shed of their home where he had been found by their five-year old son. At the inquest a year later, as reported in the Irish Examiner, Nuria told the court "My husband did not have a history of depression or other mental illness but a mild reactive depression last year. His suicide was a spur- of-the-moment action caused, I believe, by drug-induced akathisia or rapid memory turmoil. He had no say in his last decision, no choice, because his mind was overtaken by the adverse effects of SSRIs." Selective serotonin re-uptake inhibitors (SSRIs) are the latest group of anti-depressant drugs and are today the most commonly prescribed medication in Ireland. The drug Niall O'Mahony had been prescribed was Seroxat. "My husband would never have committed suicide willingly and consciously. It was against his principals, belief and character. He even rang his hospital duty office to report back to work just three days before he died" Nuria told the inquest.

No more than Joan Hamilton, Nuria is a tireless worker for reform. Working mostly on her own, she has put in many long hours of research, letter-writing and lobbying, culminating in the launch of her petition campaign entitled "We Deserve To Know the Truth about the Safety of our Prescription Drugs".

"Consumers have a right to expect full and impartial information about the potential risks and adverse effects of prescription medication. We are calling for a new robust independent regulatory framework to ensure that information is not only publicly available but also acted upon promptly. The experience of consumers must be central to a modern system for the licensing and regulation of prescription drugs and that reports of adverse reactions by consumers must be given at least as equal weight by the regulator as the chemical trials data supplied by the pharmaceutical companies. We demand such an independent safety regulatory body totally separate from the Irish Medicines Board, 100% funded by industry, to be set up for post-marketing of the drugs in Ireland funded by the State with public representation and their only mandate would be TO PROTECT THE PUBLIC. This petition also demands a mandatory clinical trial register open to all where all data is available to the public and physicians alike to make informed decisions about treatment for each individual weighing up the real risks as well as the real benefits."

MindFreedom Ireland was glad to support Nuria's petition. We provided a number of volunteers to help Nuria in Bandon Shopping Centre and later organised another day of signature gathering in Douglas Shopping Centre.

A report entitled "What We Heard" was prepared for the Expert Group on Mental Health Policy. It represented the voice of the users of the services and stated "What is worrying is the lack of information provided to patients about their medications, either in terms of the benefits or any side-effects that may be experienced. Only 24% of respondents had been given information about their medication."

In drawing attention to the role of the Irish Medicine Board, Nuria was also pin-pointing the relationship which exists between the pharmaceutical industry and the regulatory bodies. Commenting on the petition, Dr. Pat Bracken, a consultant psychiatrist at Bantry General Hospital and Clinical Director of West Cork Mental Health Services, was quoted by Susan Calnan in the Irish Times. "There are a growing number of misgivings arising among those within the medical profession in relation to the pharmaceutical industry and the way in which the industry conducts business is coming under greater scrutiny. As medical practitioners, I feel we need to become more aware of how corporate interests can sometimes dominate agendas within medicine in a way that isn't necessarily always in the best interests of patients."

We are all familiar with the recent controversy surrounding Vioxx. However, it is very encouraging to hear such statements coming from a psychiatrist. SSRIs - Seroxat, Prozac, Cipramil, Lustral, Efexor and many more- are heavily marketed to doctors and make huge profits for the companies. At the CAN conference in Cork, David Oaks had spoken about the ads for the Pfizer drug Zoloft which regularly appear on U.S.television. Jim and I had seen them when we were in California. I'm not saying and neither are Nuria or David, that these drugs cannot be of benefit to people. What we do say is that all the facts relating to them must be made available and people can then have a choice and make an informed decision for themselves.

More welcome news came from America. In an article entitled 'Big Pharma and American Psychiatry: The Good , the Bad and the Ugly' published in Psychiatric News in August 2005, Dr. Steven Sharfstein, President of the American Psychiatric Association admitted that there is "widespread concern of the over-medicalisation of mental disorders and the overuse of medications....We must examine the fact that as a profession, we have allowed the biopsychosocial model to become the bio-bio-bio model...Drug company representatives bearing gifts are frequent visitors to psychiatrists' offices and consulting rooms. We should have the wisdom and distance to call these gifts what they are - kickbacks and bribes.... If we are seen as mere pill-pushers and employees of the pharmaceutical industry, our credibility as a profession is compromised."

In responding to the article on behalf of MindFreedom, David Oaks said "Of course we welcome APA's admission that they have a drug problem. But this is too little too late." MindFreedom called for a US Congressional investigation of what they call a drug industry takeover of the mental health system. MindFreedom are right. Inform the public. Speak out. Keep up the pressure. Obviously, Dr. Sharfstein was beginning to feel it.

One brave woman who was among the first to speak out was Helena King. Helena has been caught up in the psychiatric system for over thirty years. Like me, it was after the birth of her first child that she became acquainted with it. I had first met her at Aware meetings back in the 1980's. At the time, I was totally immersed in the medical model, taking all my tablets as instructed, convinced it was the only way. But even then, Helena was a rebel. She had been introduced to the work of Peter Breggin by a friend and was already speaking out herself. Her only reason for attending the Aware meetings was for the friendship of the people she met but her anti-medication message was never welcomed. As she outlined in many letters to politicians and the media, she had been admitted to hospital on more than 60 occasions where she had been assaulted and forcibly injected. In a letter to Vincent Browne, who had taken over The Pat Kenny Show one summer, she, in her graphic and colourful style, outlined her treatment at the hands of psychiatry. It was a letter which, according to Vincent Browne himself, illicited more response than any other for the duration of the programme that summer. As I said earlier, it was Helena who had first introduced me to Peter Breggin's 'Toxic Psychiatry' but at the time, because of my drug-induced fog, I had not really appreciated its contents. But as I later began to reduce my medication and could see things in a clearer light, the book came to play an enormous role in my eventual liberation.

I became firm friends with Helena, visiting her frequently when she was in hospital and socialising with her and supporting her in the intervals she was discharged. We attended the C.A.N. conferences together where I marvelled at her ability to stand up and publicly tell it, without putting a tooth in it, like it was. She spoke of how, if she refused the drugs offered her in hospital, she literally had her arm twisted, was held down and injected into the gluteal muscle, causing her to scream in pain and being then left, broken and humiliated. Together, we went to the monthly talks organised by Joan Hamilton when she was chairperson of C.A.N. With her consent, I registered myself as her advocate with The Mental Health Commission and met with her psychiatrist. I have already mentioned how we appeared on TV3's 'Out of Sight, Out of Mind' programme. When Jim and I set up MindFreedom, Ireland, Helena was one of the first to join and one of the most active members. In June 2005, she and I, on our own and at our own expense, attended a mental health conference in Prague. For the two of us, it was an experience of mutual support and mutual empowerment made all the more so when I recalled how impossible such a trip would have been for me ten years earlier. I owe so much to Helena for all that she has helped me to achieve.

In the autumn of 2005, she found herself once again back in Carrigmor, the high security unit in Cork. If the usual practice were to be followed, she would be given a high dose of Respiridol which would cause her to sink into a prolonged depression. I decided I had to do something. Mobilising my network of contacts on the internet, I informed them all of Helena's plight. Greg White went to visit her and spoke with the nurses in charge. I received excellent advice from Tina Minkowitz, Co-Chair of the World Network of Users and Survivors of Psychiatry. She furnished me with a letter outlining the legal consequences that could follow from any breach of Helena's human rights by way of involuntary treatment. Armed with this, I made an appointment to see her psychiatrist. Over the years, Helena had been under the care of many but I had not met this man before.

In what I consider to be a definite act of attempted intimidation, two nurses asked me to go into the locked ward and down a corridor to meet the doctor in one of the adjacent rooms. Had he wanted to, he could easily have seen me in a more appropriate office near the main entrance. I had often been to visit Helena in the small, locked visiting room but this was a new, frightening experience.

As I walked down, I met some very distressed people and one, good-looking, black- haired young girl was standing at a door crying "Let me out, let me out!" over and over again. I wanted to go over and talk to her but felt this wasn't a place I could do it, while one of the nurses led me down the long, frightening corridor. This was the same corridor I had walked up and down so many years earlier when it was called St. Anne's. The staff working there now seemed not to have changed since my day. They seemed to be immune to the surroundings and how frightening it was, especially for vulnerable people. As I walked along, nobody tried to console the poor, young beautiful girl.

I was brought into the psychiatrist's room. He was flanked by a male and female nurse, neither of whom spoke. I wasn't asked if I wanted them present or not. Firstly, he quizzed me about who I was, why I was there and what organisation I belonged to. I told him I was a member of MindFreedom and C.A.N. and was a friend of Helena's for twenty years. Even though he asked some questions that were relevant to her case, I felt he wasn't really interested and didn't ask any questions to really try to understand why she always ends up in the locked unit of Carrigmor. He dismissed everything I said as only my personal experience and as such, it didn't seem to matter to him. He believed that Helena had a 'mental illness' and needed to take her medication full stop. He even suggested that I and anyone else who didn't believe in the medical model, was bad for Helena. I asked him if he had heard of Dr. Peter Breggin. He shook his head and didn't want to know. I showed him Dr. Michael Corry's book 'Depression - an Emotion not a Disease' and he would not even look at it. He was going through the motions and didn't want to hear what I had to say. I left him Tina's letter. It said

"Dear Dr. ____, I am writing to protest the treatment of Helena. Have you considered what it is like for her to be subjected to forcible injections of a mind- altering drug (haloperidol)? Are you aware that she fears this drug most of all because of the horrific adverse effects it has on her?

Such forced drugging constitutes torture according to the definitions current in international law. In particular, it is a coercive effort to change Helena against her will, based on the discriminatory judgement that she doesn't have a right to remain in a mad state or what others perceive to be a mad state.

Psychotropic drugs, particularly neuroleptics such as Haloperidol, cause profound disruption to the body, mind, emotions, identity and personality. If given to any person not considered mad, it is easily recognised as torture, diminishing the person's mental capacities and causing severe suffering. Those same drugs, if taken voluntarily, can help some people live with significant disabilities and reduce mental health crises. However, if administered involuntarily to a person who does not accept the medical approach to madness, who fears the drugs as an assault on her mind and body, it is equally torture as it would be to a person who is not mad. In fact, it may be worse since it carries a contempt and disregard for her specifically as a person who is considered mad and may be disrupting a process of madness that is actually valuable to the person."

In addition to the letter, I also left him some material pointing out that, even though the conditions and resources were poor and his job a difficult one, he ultimately was personally responsible for Helena and MindFreedom was taking note of that. I left that in writing. Experience meant very little to him. He believed what he wanted to believe from books mainly written by people who were never locked up or who had never experienced severe emotional distress. When will they ever learn? I left his room emotionally disturbed and abused all over again but was glad this time I had now been able to confront my abuser. I was able to feel the fear and do it anyway.

And in fact the visit did have some effect as Helena subsequently told me that they had held back on one of the injections and that she had noticed a change in their attitude towards her. They allowed her out for a weekend to attend a party I had to mark five years of my own freedom from the drugs and she was also allowed home for Christmas. But when she failed to report back to Carrigmor for another injection she was due, the more usual regime re-asserted itself. In what was a classic example of the brutal nature of a system devoid of respect for the dignity of a patient it was meant to be caring for, four nurses - two male and two female- accompanied by two members of An Garda Siochana, arrived at her house. Helena is a slight, 64 year old grandmother of some 9 stone. Not surprisingly, she refused to let them in and hid in a toilet. But she had been spotted and using a ladder, one of the guards gained access through an upstairs window which was open and proceded to admit the others. One of the nurses bundled a few things into a bag and within minutes, Helena was being held in the back of a car and on her way back to Carrigmor. When her friend Maria, who had been staying with her, arrived home and discovered what had happened, she rang me. I was outraged. Again, I contacted people on the internet to let them know. Two days later, I managed to speak on the phone to Helena herself. When they had taken her back, she had been forcibly injected with Halodol and also Rispiridol, and had experienced her usual terrible reaction. I felt I had to see her psychiatrist again and got on to his secretary. I was told he was too busy to see me then and would be going on holidays the following week! It was more of the arrogant treatment I had been subjected to on my first visit. Greg White went to visit Helena and subsequently posted an alert on the internet. Greg's anger was palpable. Describing what had happened, he continued: "Why all this do you think? Has Helena, a slight 64 year old grandmother, been a danger to other people, or more typically, a proselytising nuisance? Has she been a danger to herself, suicidal? No. She has merely committed the psychiatric sin of trying to make her way at home on her own without medication and not pretending otherwise.

Mary and Maria, who have known her for many years, who themselves have been there, are adamant that she is recovering from her madness. So, distraught, disgusted and dismayed, they have been trying to get an appointment with the psychiatrist behind all this, only to be told by the secretary that he is too busy to see them and anyhow, is going on leave next week.

It's extraordinary, is it not, that individuals wielding such extraordinary relative power, power to enter your house, overwhelm you, detain you and then invade your body against your will with a drug you know harms you and makes you ill; who have the power to make you so readily available for what THEY insist is care and treatment, are themselves so readily and easily unavailable to account to anyone for all this, when called to account.

If you feel as strongly about this situation as Mary and Maria and all those others who relate to her do, why not phone the secretary of the hospital and register your outrage, indignation, annoyance, curiosity, whatever you feel appropriate.

I end by quoting Krishnamurtri - 'It is no measure of health to be well adjusted to a profoundly sick society.' "

People have to speak out. These are gross violations of human rights and can not be tolerated. As John McCarthy had said at the U.C.C. conference, we have to shout out STOP, STOP, STOP.

Lydia Sapouna in U.C.C. was making her contribution too. The second in her Mental Health Forum series took place in April, 2005. The title was 'Shifting the Balance of Power in Mental Health Work - Who are the Experts?'. It was jointly organised by S.W.A.M.H. (Social Workers in Adult Mental Health) and its chairperson, Margaret Groarke. As a members of C.A.N., John McCarthy, Rose Hannon, Sinead Foley and myself were asked to speak. My talk was entitled 'A Journey from The Medical Model and I concluded my remarks by saying "The old ways have failed because power was used to control. 'They' knew what was best and insisted on doing it 'their' way. This can't work because it does not respect the dignity of the human being."

One of the other speakers on the day was Kieran Crowe. I had met Kieran a number of times before, first at a Sli Eile meeting and later at the Denmark conference with Paddy McGowan and Colette Nolan. Kieran and Paddy co-founded The Institute for Mental Health Recovery and they invited me to join them in their work. Their immediate task was to organise an international conference in conjunction with The Soteria Network, U.K. in Killarney in December, 2005. But in October, Kieran died. Everybody working for mental health reform in Ireland was shocked and saddened by the news. Kieran had been an outstanding advocate, active in many areas including the Irish Advocacy Network. He was kind and gentle, very articulate and a great inspiration and strength to me in my own journey. I know his spirit will continue to energise us all in the years ahead and it was most definitely present when the INTAR conference, attended by delegates from around the world, took place over four days in Killarney. Loren Mosher had been one of the founders of INTAR and it was an honour to have his widow, Judy present. The 'Soteria' model, the brainchild of Leon Mosher, is central to the ideals of INTAR, which is committed to exploring realistic and viable alternatives to the predominant medical model. In 'Toxic Psychiatry', Peter Breggin had described the original Soteria House. "Mosher chose a house on a busy residential street. For the staff, he sought people who had a sincere interest in listening to seemingly irrational communications of the patients. They were egalitarian and non-authoritarian individuals who didn't seek a hierarchy in which to feel superior and who didn't insist on artificial distinctions between themselves and their clients... Soteria clients gained a much better sense of self-understanding, self-esteem and personal empowerment.

instead of learning to accept brain-disabling drugs and humiliating hospitals regimes. They often can come through Soteria feeling more independent and stronger for the experience and better in touch with their feelings and aspirations." About fifty people attended the conference, survivors and professionals who saw the need for a different way. In the Soteria spirit, a non-hierarchial structure and true democratic approach marked all the proceedings. I met people I had already been in touch with on the internet and established many other new contacts. As at the WNUSP conference in Denmark, it was inspiring and exhilarating to be among such people and the small number of participants enabled a strong bonding atmosphere to develop, both during the formal day-time discussions and the more relaxed singing and dancing sessions in the bar after dinner. What was especially therapeutic for me was that I was sharing experience and knowledge with psychiatrists who understood the damage their fellow psychiatrists were doing. I was meeting true 'healers of the soul' at last.

Kieran Crowe had also begun to work closely with Dr. Pat Bracken, Clinical Director of West Cork Mental Health Services. Dr. Bracken is one of a small group of enlightened Irish psychiatrists who have had the courage to question many of the long-accepted practices of their own profession. Another one of these is Dr. Michael Corry from Dun Laoghaire. I had first become aware of him from his series of articles, The Depression Dialogues, in the Irish Times. He had also appeared on the Prime Time Investigates programme though I didn't personally know him at the time. Qualified in 1973, he worked for many years as a missionary doctor in Africa. Returning to Ireland, he further qualified as a psychiatrist and worked in St. Brendan's where he was shocked by the conditions he encountered on the back wards. In 1983, he established a Resocialisation Pilot Project to enable long-stay patients regain their place in the community but ran into such opposition, he was forced to shut it down after three years. In 1987, he founded the Institute of Psychosocial Medicine in Dun Laoghaire. On his Depression Dialogues website, he writes: "The sick brain model of depression is a hideous and terrifying concept as it turns us into cogs in a machine where, if we find the going difficult and want to disengage, we are prescribed an emotional painkiller and advised to carry on regardless." To me, Dr. Corry is the Irish version of Dr. Peter Breggin. In a letter to the Irish Times on The Report of the Inspector of Mental Health Services, he spelled out his position. "Why do psychiatrists collude with such an appalling system of care? As a psychiatrist, I can only answer for myself - fear about being the one to rock the boat. It is difficult to speak your truth when you have little or no support. Who wants to be treated as an outsider, to be labelled a rebel, a troublemaker or a whistle-blower? Who wants their misgivings about the lack of psychotherapy, the excessive use of medication, the increasingly powerful influence of the drug companies, the dangers of electro-convulsive therapy, the unconstitutionality of involuntary detention and the need for open discourse to be met with strident opposition and libel actions from colleagues? It has happened to me and it's a hideous experience."

I wanted to stand up and applaud on reading this letter and, just as I felt after reading about Dr. Terry Lynch four years earlier, I now made it my business to contact Dr. Corry personally and express my admiration and support for his brave stand. Along with his colleague Dr. Aine Tubridy, he has written a number of books including 'Going Mad', 'When Panic Attacks' and their recently published 'Depression - An Emotion not a Disease' which lives up to its claim to offer hope and understanding to those experiencing depression and does provide effective ways to create a new identity for the sufferer, rooted in self-acceptance and empowerment. Knowledge is power. For change to happen in the psychiatric world, the public need to be informed. For too long, that psychiatric world has, like the church, abused its power. The church is learning that to its cost. How long will it take for the psychiatric world to open its eyes?

Sli Eile protest.

20 HINDSIGHT.

"Hope is the thing with feathers that perches in the soul"

Emily Dickinson.

The key factor in my personal recovery was the slow reduction of my medication over the years. Gradually, my mind and spirit returned and I was able to think and feel again. But after all the years of being abused with the drugs, my body was in terrible shape. I began to walk a little every day and as my fitness improved, I increased the distance. It was difficult to motivate myself at the beginning but the more I persevered, the easier it became. At the time, I also began to attend a practical philosophy course where I discovered the importance of 'living in the now'. I began to go to the swimming pool and take part in aquarobic classes under the guidance of the inspirational Valerie. With her help, I learned how to use my whole body in the water and to love the sensation of it. I was really learning how to relax for the first time in my life and particularly re-discovered my sense of touch, a primary sense we all have at birth when we snuggle up to our mother's breast. I became more conscious too of my breathing. I realised that this was shallow which, in turn, can lead to fear and tension. Every day in the steam room, I worked on a deep breathing technique and it greatly helped me to eliminate a catarrh problem I had suffered from because of the abuse of my body over the years. It was a great feeling to know that I had achieved this myself, that I was in control over my own body. Years of psychiatric abuse had only led me to being more and more dis-empowered. All the negatives were beginning to turn into positives and I was discovering talents I never knew I possessed. I wanted to tell the whole world about the joys of my new life. Jim, Claire and Sheena began to take an interest in swimming and exercise again and many of my friends came along to join me in the pool from time to time. When I got to know Greg White, the psychotherapist from West Cork, we had lots of interesting conversations. He too had discovered the importance of breathing exercises and 'living in the now' in his own personal growth. He understood exactly my experience. His clear insights into life increased and enriched mine and mine his, I hope!

Another milestone in my recovery was knowledge. It had been ignorance that had led me into the horrific world of psychiatry and now knowledge was leading me out. I began to read. Some of the books that enlightened me were:

"Toxic Psychiatry" by Peter Breggin

"Beyond Prozac" by Terry Lynch

"Users and Abusers of Psychiatry" by Lucy Johnson

"Beyond Fear" by Dorothy Rowe

"Insanity" by Thomas Szasz

"Coming Off Psychiatric Drugs" by Peter Lehmann

"Mad in America" by Robert Whitaker

"Choice Theory" by William Glasser

"They Say You're Crazy" by Paula Caplan

"Depression - an Emotion not a Disease" by Michael Corry and Aine Tubridy

The title of this last book is excellent. It was because I was convinced by the so- called experts that I had a disease - a chemical imbalance in my brain - that I got into such trouble and lost twenty years of my life but when I discovered it was an emotion based on fear, I began my recovery. When I was deep in the 'medical model', I remember with pain my psychiatrist advising Jim to treat me "as an invalid" not realising that he was giving me a disability. I was becoming more and more dependent because of him and his 'treatment'. He was turning Jim into my carer, not my supporter. Only when I was drug free did I slowly began to regain my independence. Jim, the girls and my friends were now my supporters and I received great encouragement from them all by word of mouth and texts on my mobile phone. 'Great stuff' was a favourite of Terry Lynch and I really appreciated all the messages I received from people like Greg White, Joan Hamilton, Lydia Sapouna, Orla O'Farrell, Orla O'Donovan and Nuria O'Mahony. Pat O'Callaghan, and Brendan O'Callaghan were two other service providers who helped me greatly.

Most of all, I was supported by my fellow survivors. I had made contact with many of them at the World Conference in Denmark and through joining MindFreedom, I came into contact with many more. The internet was a tremendous asset in establishing a network around the globe and it was wonderful to feel part of such a universal movement. Jimmy McCarthy puts it very well in his song 'No Frontiers'. "When fear will lose its grip and heaven have its way." For me, fear was more and more a thing of the past. There was a time when I was scared of heights. Last summer, it gave me great pleasure to walk along Beachy Head on the south coast of England and look down, a fearless woman. The more I saw myself responsible for my own destiny and less dependent on others, the more I advanced along the road of recovery. We can choose our own recovery. It can't be forced on us for our own good. This is why forced treatments seldom work. We were born with free will and it is a necessary component in becoming strong, confident, independent human beings. Using force only increases fear and we remain dependent and unhappy. Every time "care" is forced on a vulnerable person by a service provider, it fails miserably. We need love and encouragement, not force and criticism.

It's been a long journey since that Tuesday morning in January, 1976 when it all began. Thirty long years have passed and the Cork of today, the Ireland of today have changed in many, many ways. When I think of the complicated process I had to go through to ring Sligo and Wexford with the good news that morning, it really does sound like a different century, which of course it was. I first of all had to ring the operator in Cork who then had to get through to the operator in Sligo or Wexford who in turn had to get through to Gurteen or Rosslare and even after all that, the line could suddenly just go dead.

Other things haven't changed. The little girls of Eglantine National School which our two girls attended, still wear the same green uniforms. If you drive into Sarsfield Court psychiatric hospital , everything looks exactly as it did thirty years ago, as indeed does Ward GF in Cork University Hospital. Yes, the notorious institution that was Our Lady's Hospital on the Lee Road has closed down and has been converted into luxury apartments. I often wonder do the present-day residents ever feel anything in the atmosphere, any shades of the anguish, pain, suffering and heartbreak that the long, grey, Victorian building witnessed over the years or is all forgotten as they watch their plasma TV's or gaze out their windows at the Lee, still making its silent journey from Gougane Barra all the way down to the sea.

The red brick edifice that was St. Kevin's eventually closed its doors too but not too far away, another, darker red brick building still remains. This is St. Anne's though in a Windscale/Sellafield exercise by the Southern Health Board, it is known today as Carrigmor. It is a high-security unit which underwent extensive refurbishment and renovation in recent years. Everything is clean and warm. A friendly security man will unlock the door to admit you. Inside, a prominent sign spells out a welcome, which, though well-intended, is heavily ironic. I don't know if the terrazzo steps to the first floor still remain as the only other part of the building with which I am familiar today is the small, cramped visiting room. Again, a door is unlocked to gain admission and locked again behind you. Smoking is not allowed. Two security cameras observe all from opposite ends of the claustrophobic room. A second, locked door connects to the ward inside. Functional but soul-less is how I would describe it. From what I hear, the philosophy of care inside is just the same as it was thirty years ago.

One of my abiding memories of the old St. Anne's were the Georgian style white- framed, small panel windows which could only be opened down for about six inches. I remember a November night in 1983. Only a few days earlier, Mary had had her 35th birthday. At that stage, Claire was 7 and Sheena 3. They were missing their Mom. I had gone to visit Mary as I did every evening. I can't remember what kind of form she was in that night but she was definitely the obedient patient, as she always was, taking her medication and conscientiously obeying all other directions, though she hated every minute she was spending there. I can't remember if she was due for temporary release the following weekend, as she sometimes was. She looked forward to those weekends so much. She too was missing Claire and Sheena. I said goodbye and kissed her as I always did. As I got into the car and began to drive down the avenue, I looked back. I could see Mary's face at the white-framed, small panelled window on the first floor, waving goodbye. She looked so alone and trapped. I have never forgotten that image and all its connotations.

Sadly today, some other husband could be driving down the same avenue and looking back at his wife behind what are now silver PVC windows with small vents at the top. Inside, she will queue up for her dose of Largactil just as Mary did all those years ago. If she is not aware of all the awful adverse effects of Largactil or the newer SSRI's, she too will be thinking that what she is experiencing is part and parcel of her 'illness'. If it is deemed, that after all this medication, she is not making 'progress', she could, even today in Cork, if not in Carrigmor, certainly in the psychiatric wing of the Mercy Hospital, find herself being prepared for a six to eight session course of electro-convulsive therapy. Today, we recoil in horror when we read about the terrible 'treatments' once thought acceptable to be given to patients in mental hospitals in what would now be called un-enlightened times - fifty buckets of icy water poured on the head, red hot pokers applied simultaneously to the head and feet, being rapidly spun in revolving chairs. Even in the mid- twentieth century, insulin-coma therapy which involved a drastic reduction in a patient's sugar level, resulting in coma, was a 'normal' treatment. And amazingly and scandalously, electro-convulsive therapy is still in use today.

It is a barbaric treatment. No matter how much the psychiatric establishment tries to defend its use for cases of what they call severe depression, the fact remains that it directly causes damage to the brain. Patients are assured that this is not the case, that there may be only some 'temporary' memory loss and that there is nothing to worry about. The patient may have a mild headache for a little while afterwards. Everything is played down, the current used they say is 'small' and the resultant fit 'mild'. In fact the current used can vary from 70 up to 400 volts which actually results in a 'grand mal' seizure. Before the use of anti-convulsive injections, the resulting seizures were so powerful, they frequently caused cracked vertebrae, broken bones and damaged teeth. There is something very de-humanising about ECT and what I can only describe as the callous attitude of those who administer it. Patients fears about the procedure are brushed aside. In many cases, the use of ECT is held over patients as a threat or punishment for not conforming to hospital routines or being a nuisance. It is a perfect metaphor for the control/power/domination ethos of the 'medical model'.

In the 'What We Heard' Report prepared by the late Kieran Crowe for the Mental Health Commission Expert Group, the views of the patients themselves were sought. Regarding ECT, the Report said "When asked as to whether a person had availed of ECT as a treatment, 32% said they did but of this group of people, only 53% had given informed consent to having this form of treatment." Do psychiatrists not realise the further psychological damage they inflict on their patients apart altogether from the physical damage? Would psychiatrists themselves like to be treated with so little dignity and respect? On a recent visit to University College, Cork where she spoke on the topic 'Does Mental Illness Exist?', Professor Patricia Casey stated that she would have no problem undergoing ECT herself if the need for it arose but I just wonder, I wonder.

In effect then, very little if anything, has changed over the last thirty years. The 'experts' still call the shots. The medical model is dominant, the 'chemical imbalance' theory is still propounded, depression is still a 'disease' and drugs are still the main form of treatment. More and more 'disorders' are being invented to be treated with more and more drugs, to the delight of the pharmaceutical companies whose profits grow and grow. Every year, a new crop of patients join the conveyor belt, just as we did in 1976. Pre-teen children are prescribed Ritalin. 'A pill for every ill' is becoming the norm. And yet, despite all that, a number of stark facts remain. Firstly, in America since psychotropic drugs have been used to cure 'mental illness', the numbers experiencing it have quadrupled. Secondly, in the under-developed world where there is much less use of drugs, recovery from 'schizophrenia' is twice as likely as in the drug-drenched developed world. Thirdly, in Ireland, 70% of admissions to psychiatric hospitals are re-admissions and lastly, the suicide rate in Ireland has never been higher. It is a dark picture.

But the darkest hour is just before dawn and streaks of hope have begun to appear. One of the first was Dr. Terry Lynch and his wonderful book 'Beyond Prozac'. Then came Paddy McGowan, Kieran Crowe and The Irish Advocacy Network followed by Joan Hamilton, Francis Corcoran and The Cork Advocacy Network. People like Greg White, Lydia Sapouna, Orla O'Donovan, Nuria O'Mahony, John McCarthy, Kevin McPartlan, Harry Gijbels, Rose Hannon and Asta Ghee have all made their contribution. Young blood, so vital to the cause, has emerged with Grainne Humphrys and Tim Nyhan. At a time when she was very much a lone voice, Helena King spoke out loudly and bravely and continues to do so. No more than the brave theologians who challenged their church, there are a few 'Hans Kung' psychiatrists like Dr. Michael Corry and Dr. Pat Bracken. Supporting them all is a growing international movement around the world of numerous organisations and groups, all linked by the internet, all offering mutual information and knowledge and all united in challenging the old orthodoxies. At present it is a punitive system that functions more like a criminal justice system.

What are they all campaigning for? They are working, as David Oaks of MindFreedom says, for a non-violent revolution. First of all, they want to break the silence about psychiatric oppression. They want people treated with dignity and respect. They want an end to people having their human rights abused by being locked up, forcibly drugged, electro-shocked and humiliated with psychiatric labels. They want an end to the narrow 'bio-chemical medical model' to be replaced by a more empowering holistic paradigm. They want the psychiatric profession to stand back and look at themselves and their practices. They want the voices of the abused people to be listened to and acted upon. They want to warn the public of the pervasive power of the drug companies. They want full and frank information from the drug companies so that people can make informed decisions. They want to see the establishment of small, friendly 'home' communities where people in crisis can be treated humanely. They want official recognition and some government funding for good existing alternative therapies and the public and psychiatrists to be more educated about them. They want safe places where people can go to detox from harmful psychiatric drugs.

I am proud to salute my wife Mary as one of these campaigners as are Claire and Sheena to salute their mother. I am proud to be one of these campaigners myself. As a family, we all lost a lot over the years, we all suffered in our own ways. For Mary, there was the loss of one of the most precious moments in a woman's life - the memory of the birth of her first child. There was the torture of repeated sessions of ECT, the locked wards, the separation from her family. There was the branding with stigmatising labels such as puerperal psychosis, hypomania and manic-depressive. There were the growing and worsening adverse effects she had to endure from her medication over the years - the awful akathisia, the frightening hallucin- ations, the weight gain, the hair loss, the hand tremors, the nausea, the drooling, the deadening lack of emotion which reduced her life to that of an auotmaton. There was her loss of independence, her inability to drive, her disconnection from her environment which left her totally dependent on me, with all the concomitant loss of self esteem and self-confidence. There was the dis-empowering statement from her psychiatrist that she was an 'invalid' and would have to be treated as such for the rest of her life. There was the constant fear she had to live with that failure to take her medication would have her back in hospital. There was the ultimate humiliation of being reduced from a spirited, vibrant, idealistic young woman who could move me with her playing of Beethoven's Moonlight Sonata to an abused, wrecked and hopeless middle-aged piece of psychiatric flotsam.

For Claire there was the separation from her mother in those vital early weeks and months and later for herself and Sheena, the sacrifice for all those years at an age when they were both very vulnerable, of not having their Mom around. Because Mary was so zonked with her medication and could never arise before mid-day, they didn't have her around in the mornings to make breakfast, to pack their lunches, to wrap them up for school on cold winter mornings and send them off with a hug and a kiss. There was the anxiety for them, in front of their school friends, of seeing their mother with a 'stare' in her eye, of seeing her walking with her arms held stiffly at her side, of not being completely 'with it'. There was the harsh reality for them knowing she had to take her tablets every day and even worse, that at times she was 'away' in hospital and that it wasn't just an ordinary hospital. There was the insecurity engendered when such knowledge circulated among their friends and classmates. And for me, there was the heartbreak of seeing the three most important people in my life having to suffer as they did. There was the heartbreak of seeing the joyful moment of Claire's birth being transformed into the terrible and frightening nightmare of the following days and nights and the never-to-be - erased memory of that awful drive in the ambulance in the wind and rain in through the gates of Sarsfield Court. There was the awful grim reality of the inside of those terrible institutions and of being told that Mary would have to remain incarcerated in them. There were the long drives up and down to Dublin every weekend when Mary was in St. Patrick's. There were the sad partings and the helpless feelings when her stay in hospital stretched into weeks and then into months. There were the pressures of being, at times, a single parent and having to cope with daily school work. Because of Mary's growing and ultimately total dependence on me, there was a restriction on my freedom which meant activities like school tours were out of the question. For me too, there was the shock of Mary being labelled a 'manic- depressive' and the implications that the condition, as I was told, could be genetic, though today, I am aware that such is not the case. And finally, there were those awful, scary nights when she experienced her Surmontil-induced hallucinations and I would awake, my heart thumping in fear.

It has been a long and winding road since that fateful day in 1993 when I forgot our passports. That was a catalyst but only because Mary is a brave, brave woman. It took tremendous courage. It took tremendous courage that day in Tullamore in September 2002, to stand up for the first time in front of a public audience in a crowded hotel conference room and tell her story. It took tremendous courage to appear on national television and expose herself in all her vulnerabilities. It took tremendous courage on her part to begin, in the face of the 'conventional wisdom', to begin to reduce her Largactil and ultimately cut it out. It took even more tremendous courage to begin to reduce and eventually eliminate her Lithium in the face of the threat from The Mood Disorder Fellowship of Ireland that 70% of patients "will have a major depression or manic episode within the first six months of stopping treatment."

But, as she likes to say herself, she 'felt the fear and did it anyway'. She took her courage in her hands and her reward for doing so was her liberation. She began her journey of recovery, she was born again. She discovered talents she had not known she possessed. She discovered she could write, she could swim, she could be at home on a computer. Allied to wonderful gifts of listening and counselling which she always had, she now married them all as she became an active campaigner, a fighter for human rights, a founder of MindFreedom Ireland and a humble and passionate crusader for change in the psychiatric system. Along the way she also discovered the therapeutic effects of water, music, exercise, breathing and relaxation. Mary's story is ultimately one of personal empowerment and one of hope and inspiration for others. To everybody who helped in any way along the road, and there were many,

THANKYOU.

EPILOGUE.

And so things go round and 2006, another World Cup year dawned. This time though, we were not going to have to deliberately delay any holiday to fit in with Ireland's participation in the wake of Brian Kerr's unsuccessful attempts to guide us to the finals in Germany. Disappointing as that was, the four years since 2002 and our trip to the Basque country had seen Jim and I achieve a different kind of qualification, a qualification in terms of membership of and contact with the growing international and national movements for a non-violent revolution in the psychiatric system.

One of the people I had met at the INTAR conference in Killarney was Jim Gottstein. Jim is a survivor and a qualified lawyer from Alaska who has established Psychrights, an organisation aimed at fighting the essential legal battles necessary for the non-violent revolution. I was able to link him up with MEP Kathy Sinnott as she worked on the EU Green Paper on mental health. Albeit slowly, things were beginning to happen.

In January, the Expert Group established by the Irish Mental Health Commission issued their report. Entitled 'A Vision for Change', no expense had been spared in the production of the almost 300 page glossy report which was launched in the luxurious Conrad Hotel at an event from which the Minister for Health, Mary Harney was conspicuously absent. However, in an interview on Morning Ireland, she did speak about the appaling conditions in the Central Mental Hospital, comparing them to Robben Island, the prison in Cape Town where Nelson Mandela had been locked up for nearly thirty years. To me, there are two key aspects to the whole question - one is mindset, the other money. "You get what you pay for" said Ms. Harney. 'A Vision for Change' said the same thing. "There has been much public comment in recent times about the fact that the overall share of the health budget allocated to mental health services has declined from 12% to 7% in the last twenty years. But amazingly, this is immediately followed by a recommendation that "there be a commitment to progressively increase over the next seven to ten years the pro- portion of funding given to mental health services. If the recommendations of this policy are implemented, this will increase the percentage total health fund spend on mental health to 8.24%"!!! (Exclamation marks mine).

This parsimonious attitude only serves to re-inforce the 'medical model' mindset that is still the foundation of the current psychiatric establishment. The 'chemical imbalance' philosophy which relies heavily on the use of medication can then also be buttressed by its proponents claiming a lack of funding for alternative treatments leaving them with no choice. A lack of funding was also blamed for large classes in our primary schools but rightly, it was not allowed as an excuse to continue with corporal punishment. And while not saying a great deal about the role of the pharmaceutical companies, 'A Vision for Change' did state that "one of the greatest concerns is that the influence of the pharmaceutical industry results in undue weight being put on a narrow/medical approach to mental health problems and treatments, resulting in the relative neglect of other approaches to mental health and other interventions." There were also lots of fine statements about the need "to involve service users as legitimate collaborators in their own recovery." There were proposals for the establishment of community based multi-disciplinary teams where "the contribution of each member is valued" and that a "recovery approach" should be at the heart of every level of service provision. No more than Vatican Two posing a challenge for the Catholic Church, these were challenges being set for the Irish Psychiatric establishment and its links with the pharmaceutical industry. In the U.S., brave people like Dr. Loren Mosher and Dr. Peter Breggin had been setting similar challenges for their psychiatric colleagues since the 1970's. In February, Jim and I attended the establishment of The Soteria Network in London and, at Easter 2006, Nuria and I had the privilege of meeting Peter Breggin himself when he spoke at a conference organised by Dr. Bob Johnson of The James Naylor Foundation in London. Dr. Johnson, an English psychiatrist, is of the opinion that psychiatry today is built on sand where we are all destined "to be treated as mindless unfeeling robots, gummed up by psychiatric drugs."

At the conference, we also met Dr.Michael Corry and Dr. Aine Tubridy and listened with pride as Michael told the audience about a campaign he was planning to launch in Ireland against the use of force and electro shock. He wanted to drive a stake through then heart of psychiatry, if he could find a heart! This was a message he repeated a few weeks later at the

3rd Mental Health Innovations Forum on the theme of Recovery, organised by Lydia Sapouna in U.C.C. Among the speakers was a good friend of mine, Liz Brosnan. Liz is the Resource Officer of the Western Alliance for Mental Health in Galway and shared with the audience the reported first hand experiences of people who had been in the system. Two other members of MindFreedom Ireland also spoke on the day - John McCarthy about his visit to the United Nations Convention on the Rights of Disabled People in New York and Tim Nyhan, making his public debut when delivering an excellent talk on the subject 'Finding Meaning in the Seemingly Irrational'. Also on the platform that day was the West Cork Mental Health Services Clinical Director Dr. Pat Bracken, a staunch ally of Michael Corry who displayed his enlightened thinking with a paper entitled 'Post-Psychiatry'. Dr. Corry himself facilitated a workshop which I attended on 'The Disease Model; the Real Obstacle to Recovery'.

In Charleville, Joan Hamilton and Sli Eile were still persuing their dream of establishing a Soteria-inspired house in the community. Very reluctantly, but working on the principle of taking one step back in order to take two forward, Sli Eile had to concede to the intimidating tactics of the Pike Farm Residents Association and relocate to another premises on the other side of Charleville, where, I am happy to say, there was no repeat of what had gone on in Pike Farm. It felt great to be part of a team of The Friends of Sli Eile, including Helena, as we all congregated on a Saturday morning at the end of May to do a big refit of the house, inside and out, in preparation for its proposed opening in the early autumn of 2006.

As it happened, Jim and I had decided to have our summer holiday in Germany in 2006. We had been to Bavaria a few times before but this time we spent a fortnight on the Baltic coast amid the impressive 19th century 'Baderarchitekture' of the resort of Binz on the island of Rugen. It was a holiday of sand-dunes, walks by the sea, bracing swims in the tideless waters of the Baltic and 'strandkorbe' - the quaint, traditional wickerwork two-seat shelters to be found everywhere along the low-lying coast. There was also lots of cycling, good food and plenty of dancing, the exceptionally good weather and the party atmosphere generated by Germany's progress in the World Cup all adding to the 'feelgood' atmosphere.

Being only three hours north of Berlin, we paid a visit to Peter Lehmann, secretary of ENUSP and his partner Kerstin. Both of them had been involved in the setting up of The Runaway House, one of the first Soteria-type projects to be established in Europe in the 1990's. Situated in a leafy suburb in the north of Berlin, The Runaway House is a fine example of the kind of alternative facility so badly needed today. The 2005 Report by the Irish Inspector of Mental Health Services, Dr. Teresa Carey, recognised the problem. While government policy had been to close down the large institutions and move into smaller community settings, in fact only four of these institutions had actually closed. On top of that, Dr. Carey found that the treatment regime of many patients who had been moved out into the community remained the same, with an environment that was still essentially institutional and not conducive to recovery.

As we write this epilogue Dr. Michael Corry and The Wellbeing Foundation are planning a major conference to be held in Dublin in October 2006. Entitled 'Healing Depression without Drugs or Electric Shocks', the keynote speaker will be none other that Dr. Peter Breggin himself. In his press release, Dr. Corry stated why the conference was necessary: "This conference is long overdue and reflects the current feeling that there is an urgent need for change within psychiatry. An ever-growing number of depressed individuals, their families and mental health professionals are deeply disturbed by the way depression is currently being treated. Psychiatry is attracting much criticism and anger from those using the service. Anti-psychiatry movements abound, yet none exist in other branches of medicine. Why? Because they are all accomplishing their primary task, that of delivering the best possible service. Meanwhile, on a world-wide scale there is a growing constituency of individuals who feel they have been traumatised during their treatment, who have found their emotional needs side-lined, their treatment ineffective, their difficulties with the side-effects of medication unresolved and their spirit and dignity undermined. For the majority, little or no healing occurs during psychiatric treatment, merely containment by medication, fostering in sufferers a climate of hopelessness, despair, fear and a life lived under- utilised and expressed."

The day will also include a screening of 'Soul Interrupted', a film documenting what a number of survivors have to say from North, South, East, and West. On the Sunday of the World Cup Final, I was delighted to welcome Dr. Corry and his camera man Jonathan to our house in Cork where he interviewed Nuria, John, Tim and myself, all members of MindFreedom Ireland. Two words come to mind in describing his manner - dignity and respect. Throughout everything over the last four years, those two words encapsule best of all what we survivors are seeking from the psychiatric establishment. Dr. Corry is setting an example for his colleagues. He is also challenging them to remember and return to their original mission as psychiatrists - that is to be 'healers of the soul'. As a 'soul survivor' myself, that is my fervent hope.

Incidently, the date of the Dublin conference is October 21st, the feast day of the founder of my old religious order. Maybe, after all, there is such a thing as destiny.

I am one who was abused
For 20 long years of my life
Freedom was just a word to me
Hope never to be abused again.

They took away my child
For them that was mild
They gave me shock, this has to stop
We must do all we can to block.

Not able to concentrate
Getting up far to late
Fat, slow, without much soul
They know just how to control.

Forgive them everyday
It can't be here to stay
The shock, the drugs the firm control
Destroying both heart and soul.

A chemical imbalance of the brain
The reason I was insane
Fat, slow without much soul
They know just how to control

I am one who was abused
By people who thought this was kind
Take your tablets everyday
Then life will work out just fine

Many people in the world are abused
Their souls are locked and chained
Happiness is just a word to them
I hope some day they'll be FREE.

LET US KNOW HOW TO SING
LAUGH, DANCE AND TO SMILE
LET US KNOW, FEEL JOY AND LOVE
I HOPE SOMEDAY WE'LL BE FREE.

I know one day we'll be free

Mary   Maddock

The head floated on the bed,
disembodied, this was a mental hospital,
no need for the body,
treatment could and would be confined to the mind,
The room was pleasant clean,
bed, wardrobe, to hang a hat so it was small,
en-suite, washbasin, mirror,
shelf for toilet or shower,
ecomically, ergonomically, viable.

The head was sad, depressed,
hence the hospital,
journey began with a visit to the GP.
"Please help me". What's the problem,
sprain, pain, come on explain,"
"I am depressed," said the head.
"Oh not my area, I can't hear yea.

The head on a couch, Mr. in a chair,
"I am here I care, what are you thinking?
I can hear it clinking, your mental motor,
express your feelings, expand be profound"
"I want it to end, to be final",
"Hold that thought; stop right there,"
he jumped from the chair" I will admit yea, commit yea."

The head in admittance, talking to junior,

your details, past future, "HURRUMPH

Do you have V.H.I?

Oh good, plan B private ward whoopee".

Into the lift give a shift, multi coloured tablets,

smarties,

the haze, daze blurred vision, brain neutral,

you'll be fine now, neutered, no control,

sleep, eat, do not think,

doctor calls, pops in the door, does his best to ignore.

"how is he? Goohood, then I will see him tomorrow".

The head knows when he is to see the Mr.

the quiet expectation of the staff,

the gathering of the doctors nurses whispers,

they all bow and scrape as he floats in on his cape,

God is in his heaven, attended by his acolytes and

high priestesses.

The door opens the Mr in the cape the rest gather and gape,

"How is he, better decrease by 25?"

"How is he, worse then increase by 75?"

gasps of astonishment, acknowledgement.

The head is ignored.

The head is on the bed, solitary,

the head is clear, without care,

the smarties under the pillow,

the plan is forming, I will go in the morning,

just roll down the stairs, apples and pears.

He will greet the dawning, while they are all

yawning,

Hit the street do a streak,

faster, faster, cry freedom,

free at last, free at last,

I beat um, I beat um.

John Mc Carthy

Schizophrenia

Wise as a serpent, my love
Gentle as a dove
You are a hand that gives
A heart that holds
Some pain, some beauty
Some terror, some divinity
Your life is to be lived, my love

Sedation, seduction
Creation, destruction
Rejection, perfection
A new direction
Your medication
Is three tablets a day
Of hope and love and trust

This combination, concoction, finely-tuned cocktail
Of acceptance, receptiveness and openness
To free, share, own and know
The terrible beauty and turbulence of your mind
To own and honor it
Your dangerous gift
To respect it's impact
To name it, know the facts
Your kaleidoscopic mind, hallucinogenic kind

Delusions, illusions

Relapse, collapse

Inside your shattered self

Is you, gentle as a dove

Full of love

Someone I feel comfortable with

You are blessed with

Heart consciousness

Your open heart

Has helped me to see

Yet you are not free

Living a half-life of corridors

Blocked by major neuroleptics

And sets of keys

Are you fed up being the subject of intense scrutiny

Objectified, petrified

Separated, feeling persecuted

Isolated

Labeled, when all you want

Is to be cradled

When care becomes control, contain

An inner landscape all of your own

A wild dog you must tame

A dangerous gift you must name

Psychic powers to be reined in

The emotional pain that drives you insane

Schizophrenia, it's just a word
What does it mean?
Demystify this diagnosis, this life sentence
It is split from reality
Not split personality
It is loaded with bullets of discrimination
Dopamine levels, frontal lobes
Neurotransmitter nonsense

Thinking outside the box
Bizarre behaviour, spiritual saviour
Poetic metaphor to reveal trauma, neglect and conflict
Perception, rejection, projection
What is the meaning of life?
Poet, philosopher
Between the worlds, spirits, ghosts
Do you hear voices?
If you do, do you have choices?
Since when has emotional vulnerability, a strength
Become a chemical imbalance?
A broken heart, sensitivity, fragility
Emotional distress, identity crisis
A crime?

Grainne Humphreys

Recommended Reading:

'Toxic Psychiatry' by Dr. Peter Breggin, Harper Collins, London, 1993. In a searing, mind-shattering exposition, Dr.Breggin bursts through the hype surrounding the 'New Psychiatry' and shows how dangerous, even potentially brain-damaging, many of its drugs and other treatments are. The book is a cornerstone of psychiatric human rights literature. '

Beyond Prozac' by Dr. Terry Lynch, Mercier Press, Cork, 2005. In this controversial, deeply-felt and hard-hitting book, Dr. Terry Lynch takes issue with conventional medical treatment of psychiatric or emotional problems. He questions how doctors diagnose different levels of emotional disturbance and the efficacy - and inherent dangers - of the drug therapies that are offered to many people as a matter of course.

'Mad in America' by Robert Whitaker, Perseus Publishing, Cambridge, Massachusetts, 2002. This book presents an insightful, courageous expose of how madness went from 'out of sight, out of mind' to be a source of massive corporate profits. A must-read for anyone with a friend or family-member labelled 'mentally ill', for psychiatric survivors, mental health professionals and those interested in the corporate buy-out of a profession.

'Users and Abusers of Psychiatry' by Lucy Johnson, Routledge, London, 2000. This is a radically different, critical account of the day to day practice of psychiatry. Using real life examples and her own experience as a clinical psychologist, Lucy Johnson argues that the traditional way of treating mental breakdown can often exacerbate peoples' original difficulties leaving them powerless, disabled and even more distressed.

'Unsafe at any Dose' by Dr. Bob Johnson, Trust Consent Publishing, Isle of Wight, 2006. If you want to know how psychiatry is built on sand and how highly trained men and women can ignore irrefutable scientific proof that psychiatric drugs do more harm than good, this is the book for you.

'Medicines out of Control?' by Charles Medawar and Anita Hardon, Aksant Publishing, Amsterdam, 2004. This book is mainly about the control and consumption of mood-altering drugs and the systematic fiddling of the accounts of drug benefit and risk.

'Beyond Fear' by Dorothy Rowe, HarperCollins, London, 2002.
This is a comprehensive study of how the 'mentally ill' are still regarded as inferior and dangerous and, under the guise of care, are often treated inhumanely and sometimes very cruelly. Recognising fear as a desperate emotion of defence in what psychiatrists call 'mental disorders', Dorothy Rowe argues that by knowing ourselves, we can go beyond our fear and face life with courage.

'They Say Your're Crazy' by Paula J. Caplan, Addison-Wesley, New York, 1995. A critical look at the DSM (The Diagnostic and Statistical Manual of Mental Disorders), the bible of the American Psychiatric Association.
Paula Caplan demonstrates that much of what are labelled 'mental disorders' are actually common life problems or the effects of social injustice.

'Insanity - The Idea and Its Consequences' by Thomas Szasz, Syracuse University Press, New York, 1997.
Renowned dissident psychiatrist Dr. Szasz challenges the way both science and society define insanity. Insanity, he says, is not a disease with origins to be excavated but a behaviour with meanings to be decoded.

'Depression: An Emotion not a Disease' by Dr. Michael Corry and Dr. Aine Tubridy, Mercier Press, Cork, 2005.
Depression, the authors assert, is an emotion just like fear, anger or love which can be consciously influenced, rather than a disease which can be suffered. This approach promises to end the cycle of relapse, medication and possible hospitalisation. It puts the sufferer back in the centre of a more individual and tailored approach to healing and it raises crucial questions about the medical community's focus on medication as primary treatment.

'Coming off Psychiatric Drugs' by Peter Lehmann, Peter Lehmann Publishing. Berlin, 2004.
In "Coming off Psychiatric Drugs" 28 people from Australia, Austria, Belgium, Denmark, England, Germany, Hungry, Japan, the Netherlands, New Zealand, Sweden, Switzerland and the USA write about their experiences with withdrawal. Additionally, eight professionals, working in psychotherapy, medicine, social work, psychiatry, natural healing and a runaway-house, report on how they helped in the withdrawal process.

Important Websites:

http://www.mindfreedom.org

http://www.szasz.com

http://www.breggin.com

http://www.moshersoteria.com

http://www.narpa.org

http://www.drugawareness.org/home.html

http://www.aspire.us

http://www.ahrp.org

http://www.psychrights.org

http://www.soteria-alaska.com

http://www.depressiondialogues.ie

http://www.peter-lehmann-publishing.com/withdraw.htm

http://prawn.sarlorelli.gen.nz

http://www.benzo.org.uk/prawn.htm

http://www.beyondthepsychiatricbox.blogspot.com

http://www.dorothyrowe.com.au

http://www.asylumonline.net

MindFreedom Mission Statement

"In a spirit of mutual co-operation, MindFreedom leads a non-violent revolution of freedom, equality, truth and human rights that unites people affected by the mental health system with movements for justice everywhere."

Does Mental illness exist

The Great Mental Illness Con
If mental illness is a disease, a biochemical event, there must be:

1.   Reliable evidence of a consistent cause-effect relationship between Schizophrenia, BAD, Depression, PTSD, ADHD etc and a brain disorder such as lesion, tumour, microbes or other markers.

2.   Evidence of a reliable diagnostic scan or test of brain, blood, urine, genes, etc that can distinguish untreated individuals with diagnoses from individuals without them.

3.   Evidence of a base-line standard, chemically balanced "normal" personality against which imbalance can be measured and shown corrected by pharmaceutical means.

4.   Evidence psychotropic drugs can reliably correct, heal, or cure such imbalance Lacking such evidence claims that emotional distress equals mental illness are unsustainable

NB: It is generally recognised that most psychotropic medication andother interventions are linked to harmful side effects and damaging structural brain changes - often permanent. Published information has frequently been shown to conceal or down-play such evidence

CASL
The Campaign
for Abolition of the Schizophrenia Label

CASL was launched on 6th September 2006 at a conference in Manchester to celebrate the 20th anniversary of Asylum magazine, the 15th anniversary of the Hearing Voices Network and the 12th anniversary of Psychology Politics Resistance (PPR). The canpaign is driven by two central factors:

1) The concept of schizophrenia is unscientific and has outlived any usefulness it may once have claimed.

2) The label schizophrenia is extremely damaging to those to whom it is applied.

The idea that schizophrenia can viewed as a specific, genetically determined, biologically driven, brain disease has been based on bad science and social control since its inception. Indeed few scientists represent themselves as happy with the illness model and increasingly it is only seen to serve the interests of the pharmaceutical industry's voracious appetite for control of human experience. It is also harmful because the diagnostic process makes it impossible to make sense of the problems that lay at the roots of people's distress. The scandal is that in the 21st century intelligent human beings are deemed to be `lacking insight' for questioning a label proven to lack scientific validity.

Experience gained through many years of working with individuals labelled with schizophrenia and their families, is that the question of scientific validity and reliability in relation to schizophrenia is a secondary problem. The main problem is the appalling level of stigma attached to this label. To be labelled 'a schizophrenic' is one of the most devastating things that can happen to anyone. The label implies dangerousness, unpredictability, chronic illness, inability to work or function and a lifelong need for medication that will often be ineffective but will usually cause unpleasant side effects. Lives are being ruined on the basis of a highly suspect diagnostic system.

We now know that the mayor complaints of 'schizophrenia' are rooted in daily life problems like traumatic experience and identity crisis but these are mystified using the schizophrenia concept. We believe the time is ripe for a paradigm shift across the field of mental distress and that the alternative knowledge and resources are now in place to mobilise for change. We are convinced that the future health of communities lies largely in the hands of organisations like the Hearing Voices Network and new initiatives like the Paranoia Network and Depression Dialogues.

CASL's strategy is to take the professional and scientific evidence against the schizophrenia label into local communities where it really counts. We are working to build a broad coalition of service users groups and like minded professionals, with the aim of bringing a more coherent and humane diagnostic system to service users worldwide. Above all the organisers and supporters of the campaign know that there are real alternatives to the schizophrenia concept.

The campaign co-ordinating group:
Peter Bullimore, Jacqui Dillon, Paul Hammersley, Terence McLaughlin, Marius Romme.
Contact castle@asylumonline.net visit http://www.asylumonline.net

The CASL campaign is led by Asylum: an international magazine for democratic psychiatry, psychology, education and community development.

SUBSCRIBE TO *Asylum*

Cost
UK £12 for 4 issues
(£24 for large organisations)
Europe £16,
International £18 for 4 issues

Make cheques payable to:
Asylum

Send to:
Asylum Associates
Limbrick Centre, Limbrick Rd, Sheffield S6 2PE
subs@asylumonline.net

Name

Organisation

Address

Postcode   email **(Optional)**

Asylum is owned entirely by its readers. It is produced by Asylum
Associates a not-for-profit workers co-operative and edited by an
international collective. Visit http://www.asylumonline.net

ORDER
'STRONGER THAN EVER'

The Report of the First Survivor Worker Conference UK
by Rose Snow

PUBLISHED BY ASYLUM

Price for individuals and small groups **£4** uk

£5 Europe

£6 International

Large organisations **£24.97**

MAKE CHEQUES PAYABLE TO: Asylum

SEND TO:

Asylum Associates, Limbrick Centre, Limbrick Rd, Sheffield S6 2PE

Name _____

Organisation _____

Address _____

_____

_____

_____

Postcode _____   email **(Optional)** _____

ORDER
PAINTING
THE
RAINBOW

BY WAYNE D CLAY

PUBLISHED BY ASYLUM
COST UK £6,
EUROPE £7,
INTERNATIONAL £8

A STORY TO MAKE YOU LAUGH
AND CRY AND LAUGH AGAIN

MAKE CHEQUES PAYABLE
TO: Asylum

SEND TO: Asylum Associates
Limbrick Centre, Limbrick Rd,
Sheffield S6 2PE

Name _____

Organisation _____

Address _____

_____

_____

_____

_____

Postcode _____ email *(Optional)* _____